A
HERO
FOR THE
AMERICAS

"Statue of Gonzalo Guerrero by Raul Ayala Arellano, 1974" by Feliks, 2008 (original in colour). Used under a Creative Commons licence.

A HERO FOR THE AMERICAS

The Legend of Gonzalo Guerrero

ROBERT CALDER

University of Regina Press

Printed and bound in Canada at Friesens. The text of this book is printed on 100% post-consumer recycled paper with earth-friendly vegetable-based inks.

Cover design: Duncan Campbell, University of Regina Press
Text design: John van der Woude, JVDW Designs
Copy editor: Dallas Harrison
Proofreader: Kristine Douaud
Indexer: Sergey Lobachev, Brookfield Indexing Services
Cover art: Detail of sculpture by Carlos Terrés. "Allegory of mestizaje," 1981, terroca and reinforced concrete, 35 x 19 m, City of Chetumal Quintana Roo. Used with permission.

Library and Archives Canada Cataloguing in Publication

Calder, Robert Lorin, 1941-, author
    A hero for the Americas : the legend of Gonzalo Guerrero / Robert Calder.

Includes bibliographical references and index. Issued in print and electronic formats. ISBN 978-0-88977-509-1 (softcover).—ISBN 978-0-88977-510-7 (PDF).—ISBN 978-0-88977-511-4 (HTML)

1. Guerrero, Gonzalo, -approximately 1528. 2. Spaniards—Mexico—Biography. 3. Shipwreck victims—Mexico—Biography. 4. Mayas—Mexico—History. 5. Mexico—History—Conquest, 1519-1540. 6. Yucatán Peninsula—History. I. Title.

F1435.C35 2017   972'.02092   C2017-905023-0   C2017-905024-9

10 9 8 7 6 5 4 3 2 1

University of Regina Press, University of Regina
Regina, Saskatchewan, Canada, S4S 0A2
tel: (306) 585-4758 fax: (306) 585-4699
web: www.uofrpress.ca

We acknowledge the support of the Canada Council for the Arts for our publishing program. We acknowledge the financial support of the Government of Canada. / Nous reconnaissons l'appui financier du gouvernement du Canada. This publication was made possible with support from Creative Saskatchewan's Creative Industries Production Grant Program.

For Holly

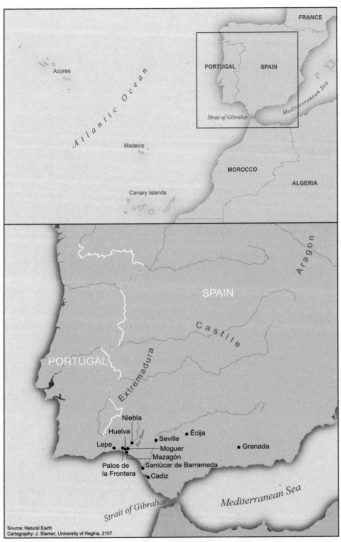

Map 1. Spain

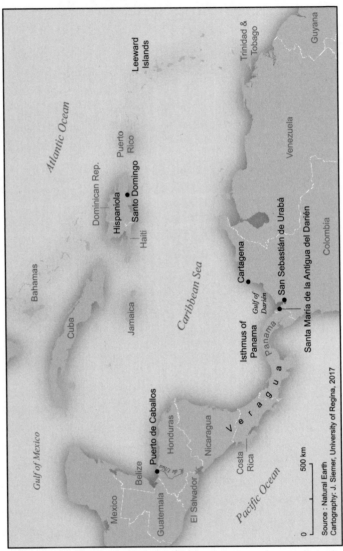

Map 2. The Caribbean

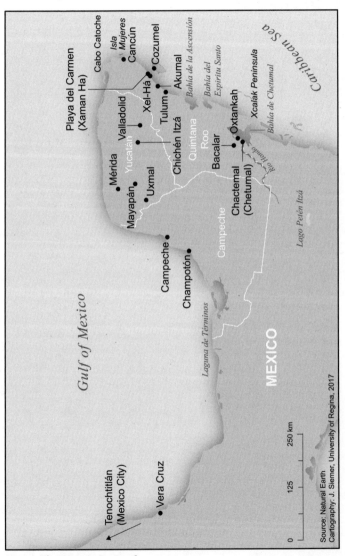

Map 3. The Yucatán Peninsula

"A Haunting, Tantalizing Tale"

In January 1512, a mere twenty years after Christopher Columbus first saw the New World, a party of Spanish men and women were shipwrecked while sailing from what is now Panama to Hispaniola (the island comprising Haiti and the Dominican Republic). About twenty survivors were blown onto the Yucatán Peninsula, the first Europeans to set foot on that soil, and they were soon captured by its inhabitants, the Maya. The castaways' leaders, according to the common practice in Mesoamerica, were sacrificed to the Mayan gods, and all but two of the remaining party died from the effects of their days at sea and their subsequent enslavement.

The fate of this shipwrecked company remained a mystery to Spanish colonial officials until 1519, when the conquistador Hernán Cortés landed on Cozumel Island, off the Yucatán coast, at the beginning of his great trek into the heart of Mexico. Out of the jungle emerged a Spaniard, Jerónimo de Aguilar, who spoke of his seven years of captivity in a Mayan tribe and of his great joy at being reunited with his countrymen. He also spoke of another Spaniard, whom he called Gonzalo, who likewise had learned of the presence of Spanish ships at Cozumel but had declined to join Aguilar in seeking them. Gonzalo, he said, had risen from slave to military captain in a Mayan tribe, had married the daughter of the chief, and had fathered three children. Moreover, he had adopted the native customs and beliefs so thoroughly that he could never again live among his own people.

Aguilar remained with Cortés's company and, serving as one of the most famous translators in Mesoamerican history, became an essential part of the remarkable conquest of Montezuma's Aztec Empire. As a reward for his services, he was given sizable tracts of land and numerous native tenants near Mexico City, and his name appears frequently in the historical accounts of sixteenth-century Spanish chroniclers. Aguilar left no memoirs or letters, though he submitted several petitions to the Spanish court near the end of his life, so his attitudes and motivations will never be fully understood.

Although something of his life in Yucatán and mainland Mexico is known, Gonzalo remains a mysterious figure. Like Aguilar, he gave no written account of his life, but unlike Aguilar he left no trace of himself in any civic or legal proceedings. He exists as a historical figure because of the testimony of Aguilar, the only Spaniard known to have seen him after the shipwreck; the subsequent accounts of chroniclers, notably Bernal Díaz del Castillo, Gonzalo Fernández de Oviedo, Francisco López de Gómara, Fray Diego de Landa, and Francisco Cervantes de Salazar; and an intriguing letter to the Spanish government from a colonial official in Honduras in 1536, a report of the body of a Spaniard found on a battlefield among the native dead.

Some current historians believe that Gonzalo never existed, that he was invented by Aguilar to enhance his stature by embodying everything that he was not: an apostate to Aguilar's unshakable faith, a cohabiter with a pagan woman to Aguilar's resolute chastity, and a traitor to his countrymen to Aguilar's steadfast loyalty. The chroniclers, the argument goes, seized on the Gonzalo story, embellishing it in their own ways to explain away an embarrassing fact: whereas it took Cortés less than three years to destroy the extensive Aztec empire, the Spanish needed more than two decades to subjugate the Yucatán Peninsula. The unpalatable conclusion that the Maya were more determined than the Spanish and capable warriors led by shrewd native military strategists could be set aside if the Mayan resistance was seen in fact to have been led by a Spaniard. Hence the appellation of Gonzalo Guerrero (i.e., "warrior"), given by López de Gómara, to the shipwrecked sailor previously known only as Gonzalo.

Despite the paucity of firm historical evidence of the existence of Gonzalo Guerrero—or perhaps because of the ambiguity surrounding him—the succeeding centuries have seen him become, in the words of Rolena Adorno, Reuben Post Halleck Professor of Spanish and Portugese at Yale University, "one of the remarkable...phenomena of Spanish-Conquest-era historiography."[1] On the Yucatán Peninsula today, there are at least four statues of him, all imposing representations of a powerful figure dressed as a Mayan warrior but surrounded by his Mayan wife and their Spanish-Mayan children. They are prominently mounted in the village of Akumal along the east coast, on the main avenue running along the shore of Cozumel Island, at the centre of one of the most important intersections in the city of Mérida, and at the main entry to the region's other large centre, Chetumal. Buildings, streets, and lagoons bear his name, and murals and paintings in government buildings depict the story of his becoming a native warrior and the father of a Mayan family. A suburb of Mérida and a district of Playa del Carmen are called Gonzalo Guerrero, rooms at the University of Quintana Roo in Chetumal are named after him and his Mayan wife, and every year a prestigious arts fellowship is awarded in his name in that city.

A body of literature, both fictional and scholarly, has also begun to grow around the legend of Guerrero. In the late twentieth century, poets and fiction writers became fascinated by the tale of the Spaniard-turned-Maya (and of his fellow castaway

Aguilar, without whom the story is incomplete), and—like the sixteenth-century chroniclers—they elaborated, amended, and reinterpreted the narrative. Inevitably, several texts were published in Mexico that purported to be the recently unearthed memoirs of Guerrero hidden for centuries, but, as Adorno points out, they are implausible, though interesting for their celebration of him as a Mayan patriot and creator of Mexican *mestizaje*, the blending of European and indigenous Central American races. Guerrero, too, has been given the twenty-first century's ultimate recognition of status in international popular culture: his own website.

Guerrero has thus become a legend far beyond the bare bones of historical documentation, a figure who represents some fundamental and fascinating elements in the story of the Spanish conquest and the creation of modern Mexico. In this, he is like other legends celebrated far beyond the sparse historical facts of their lives: Spartacus, the first-century BCE slave who became a symbol of rebellion against tyranny; King Arthur, whose Knights of the Round Table came to represent courtly ideals; and Robin of Locksley, who as Robin Hood embodied the common people's resistance to the wealthy and the politically corrupt.

The conquest of Mexico has spawned legends and myths around key figures in the story—even those, such as Montezuma, about whom there is substantial historical documentation. The Mexican poet Octavio Paz has written that the "strange permanence" of Hernán Cortés and his native translator/mistress Malinche in "the Mexican's imagination and sensibilities reveals that they are something more than historical figures: they are symbols of a secret conflict that we still have not resolved."[2] The legend of Malinche, or Marina as she was known to the Spanish, became so embedded in Mexican culture that in the twentieth century the common perception of her part in the conquest gave rise to the contemptuous term *malinchista*.

The legendary and symbolic meanings of Cortés have been built on a substantial body of documents: Spanish court records, the conquistador's own reports, and the writings of a number of sixteenth-century chroniclers. Our knowledge and understanding of Malinche, however, are based upon much less: two brief references to her in Cortés's reports and occasional mentions by the chroniclers, most of whom wrote years after her death, often an ocean away from Mexico and driven by particular biases.

"Certainty," writes Camilla Townsend, "is elusive,"[3] and until her book *Malintzin's Choices* there was—despite thousands of pages of fiction, poetry, and anthropological, cultural, and feminist studies—no scholarly biography. The explanation for this absence, says Townsend, is simple: "There is probably only one compelling reason why a traditional biography of Malinche was not written years ago; that it cannot be done. The evidence simply does not exist to write such a book. The woman left us no diaries or letters, not a single page."[4] Townsend has nonetheless written a provocative and scholarly book about a figure who "was catapulted to the very center of the drama of two continents colliding,"[5] and she has done so by providing "full details on every aspect of Malinche's context and [placing] her actions in their proper setting, allowing readers to see what kind of thoughts she might have entertained in such a situation, as well as the extent to which her actions mattered.... What I tried to write, then, is a book about contexts."[6] The strategy here was to create a vivid and detailed picture of her subject's background and context and, by doing so, to outline the figure in the foreground. Much of that portrait must necessarily be speculative, but it nonetheless sheds light on important matters such as the nature of the interaction between the Spanish invaders and the indigenous peoples, the parts played by native women in this interaction, and the contributions to Mexican historical consciousness of those caught in the clash of two worlds.

Much of what Townsend says about Malinche's place in the history of the conquest and about a strategy to understand who Malinche really was and what she represented can also be said about Gonzalo Guerrero. If one assumes, as I do, that a Spanish sailor named Gonzalo really was shipwrecked along the Yucatán coast in 1512 and lived among the Maya for several decades, then his story is remarkable. It is the story of a Castilian coming of age during the birth of Spain as a nation, a time of tumultuous upheaval within the country, and a period of astonishing discoveries of unimagined new lands and peoples across the Atlantic. It is the story of a young adventurer who worked for two of Spain's greatest conquistadors—Vasco Núñez de Balboa and Francisco Pizarro—in Darién, the first European settlement ever built on the mainland of the Americas. It is the tale of a shipwrecked sailor, captured by the Maya in Yucatán, who declined to join another extraordinary conquistador, Hernán Cortés, and so missed being part of one of the most remarkable conquests in history. It is the tale of a man born and raised as a sailor and a Catholic in Castile who became a Mayan warrior and the father of the first mixed-race children in Mexican history. It is the story of a Spaniard who, as a military leader of Yucatán natives for two decades, thwarted the colonizing dreams of yet another eminent conquistador, Francisco de Montejo, and then was felled in battle by Pedro de Alvarado, notorious for being the most brutal of the Spanish conquerors of the Aztecs. It is, says Adorno, "a haunting, tantalizing tale, marked by its tellers with transgression in every conceivable variant: sexual, religious, cultural, and political; Gonzalo Guerrero variously embodies lasciviousness, miscegenation, apostasy, heresy, military valor, and treason."[7]

This book offers a narrative of Guerrero's transformation from conventional young Castilian to Mayan tribesman and warrior and ultimately to his death on the battlefield. Given the absence of extensive archival material, I have tried to suggest how remarkable such a transformation would have been for someone caught in the confrontation between the old European world and the new American world. As much as possible, I have avoided ascribing intentions and emotions to Guerrero; having, I hope, helped readers to trace his path through the tumultuous and quickly changing life of fifteenth- and sixteenth-century Spain and of the New World, I leave it to them to infer how he might have found his way emotionally and intellectually. However they ultimately see Guerrero, his story—man or myth—is an important element of the history of Mexico. It is, moreover, part of the broader fabric of the European encounter with the Americas and the violence and accommodation that resulted from this meeting.

CHAPTER ONE

"No White Man Ever Enters It":
THE YUCATÁN PENINSULA

When you walk through the colourful archway that is the entrance to the Mexican seaside village of Akumal, you cannot avoid seeing Gonzalo Guerrero. A defiant figure set on a stone plinth, one hand clutching a spear and the other cradling the head of a small boy, he seems to challenge the multitude of visitors who—wearing shorts, gaudy shirts, and floppy hats and armed with swim fins and snorkel masks—are eager to get to the beach beyond. Were he to come to life, he would be baffled by their presence and appearance, but in the faces of the locals who greet and serve them he might well recognize the descendants of the indigenous people, the Maya, who transformed his life five centuries earlier.

Akumal is situated on the Yucatán Peninsula, on what the enterprising Mexican government has given the sexy name of the Mayan Riviera, a strip of shoreline running 160 kilometres from the resort city of Cancún south to the ancient coastal ruins of Tulum. For more than a decade, this stretch of beach, coral reef, and lagoon has been the fastest growing, most transformed tourist haunt in the world. Every year about 7 million tourists fly into Cancún, and hundreds of thousands more will land at an international airport soon to be built near Tulum.

The Yucatán Peninsula has been the home of the Maya for more than 1,500 years, and glimpses of their rich cultural heritage are woven into the tourist experience. All of the major hotels sport Mayan motifs, and in the evenings many offer dramatic tableaux performed by local actors in feathers, leathers, and sandals, looking as if they have wandered in off the set of Mel Gibson's histrionic film about Mayan bloodletting, *Apocalypto*. Tour companies take visitors to three of the peninsula's great Mayan ruin sites—Chichén Itzá, Coba, and Tulum—where, in a three-hour outing, they are given the basic facts of Mayan history, architecture, cosmology, religion, and numerology. Most tourists come away happier to have climbed a pyramid or looked into the murky waters of a *cenote*, a "sinkhole," and thrill to the idea of virginal girls being hurled into it to appease ancient gods.

Once in a while, when a tourist has looked around at such magnificent ruins, most of them only partially uncovered and restored and promising so much more under the jungle foliage, he or she will turn to the guide and ask, "What happened to the Mayans? Where did they go?" If the guide is indigenous, in this case short in stature, dark-complexioned, black-haired, and ebony-eyed, with high cheekbones and perhaps a prominent curved nose, he is likely to laugh and, hiding a slight contempt because there is a tip at stake, reply, "We haven't gone anywhere. We're still here where we've always been."

Few tourists recognize that the guide who stands before them, the waiter who serves them in the hotel dining room, or the taxi driver who hustles them into Playa del Carmen is likely descended from the Maya who produced the architectural wonders that they have been seeing. Even fewer realize that they might be looking at a descendant of the striking figure in the statue, Gonzalo Guerrero.

Nor are many travellers likely to be aware that the oval or rectangular buildings constructed with poles and thatched roofs and a door at each end that they see in so many villages as they drive through the countryside are the same structures—called the *na*—that housed ordinary Maya 1,000 years earlier. And that many of the people whom they see tending a cottage industry or simply maintaining a farm and a garden, called for centuries a *milpa*, in the interior of the peninsula speak Maya first and then perhaps Spanish.

Tourists who fly into Cancún for a week or two of sunshine and sybaritic life see themselves having a Mexican holiday, and, as long as they remain in the homogenized tourist belt, they encounter little to suggest otherwise. Engage permanent residents in lengthy conversations, however, and whether they are sixth generation or first they will soon let you know that they are Yucatán first and Mexican second. Among many of its people, the Yucatán Peninsula is called La Hermana República de Mexico, "the Sister Republic of Mexico." This is not merely local pride; geographically and culturally, the peninsula could well have become an independent nation. And its long, tumultuous, and violent history, from Gonzalo Guerrero's day to the middle of the twentieth century, nearly made it one.

Geographically and politically, the Yucatán Peninsula has always been essentially separated from the rest of Mexico. A large thumb of land thrust north and east out of southern Mexico, it is connected to the mainland by a narrow neck of land made up of low swamp and dense jungle. The rigours of crossing this terrain—there was no regular-gauge railway or highway until the late 1950s—meant that for centuries communication and travel between Yucatán and the mainland had to be conducted over water. Before the arrival of the Spanish in the early sixteenth century, this challenging land bridge offered the Maya of the Yucatán some defence against the power of the México (Aztec) Empire, the centre of which was the great city of Tenochtitlán, on the present site of Mexico City. While the communities within easier reach of

Tenochtitlán were expected to pay annual tributes to the central government, provide slaves when required, and fight alongside the Aztec forces should the empire be threatened, the Yucatán Maya were essentially at the outer edge of Tenochtitlán's influence. This isolation was especially important after the collapse of the great Mayan city-states around 900 CE rendered their component social groups much more vulnerable to external forces.

When, following Columbus's reaching the New World in 1492, the Spanish began to explore the Caribbean, their first significant and enduring contact with continental North America, in 1517, was with the Yucatán Peninsula when Francisco Hernández de Córdoba led an expedition from what is now Cuba to look for slaves and new territories. After landing at Isla Mujeres, a small sliver of land off the northeastern coast, he moved west to Cabo Catoche, where his men fought with a band of local inhabitants, and, after some further exploration along the coast, he returned to Cuba. The following year Juan de Grijalva landed on Cozumel and, from a distance, saw first a settlement at Xel-Há and then ruins so impressive that they were surely those of Tulum. "Almost at sunset," wrote the accompanying missionary Juan Díaz, "we saw in the distance a town or village so large that the city of Seville could not be better or larger; and in it could be seen a very large tower. Many Indians were running along the shore with two banners which they raised and lowered."[1] Finally, in 1519, Hernán Cortés led an expedition that landed at Cozumel and then sailed around the peninsula to begin a remarkable march into the heart of the Aztec Empire.

Few conquests in the history of the world have been as swift or dramatic as that of Cortés's capturing of this empire. With little more than 500 men, some horses, and some cannons, as well as a great deal of diplomatic guile and treachery (the Aztec emperor, Montezuma II, was long believed to be a naive, superstitious, and foolish opponent), Cortés was able to defeat an enemy that outnumbered him by a factor of something like 200-1. At the time that he attacked Tenochtitlán, the city itself is estimated to have held 150,000 people. But, as Ronald Wright has pointed out, Cortés had a weapon against which the Aztecs had no defence, a biological weapon that "utterly transformed the balance of power."[2] In the midst of the Spanish assault, smallpox, brought to the New World by Europeans, ravaged indigenous peoples, causing one Spanish friar to observe of the Aztecs that "more than one half of the population died. They died in heaps, like bedbugs."[3] Thus aided by biology, Cortés conquered the Aztec kingdom only thirty months after he landed at Cozumel.

Defeating the Maya and taking control of Yucatán, however, proved to be much more difficult even though they too had suffered terribly from the effects of smallpox. In 1526, one of Cortés's conquistadors, Francisco de Montejo, was charged with the task, but it was almost twenty years and another generation of leaders before the Spanish could claim control of most of the peninsula. Not only was the terrain difficult, but also Montejo and his successors did not face an opponent as trusting as Montezuma, who believed that the Spanish were gods who had returned from the east, as had long been prophesied in Mesoamerica. The Maya were not so deceived: they knew that their invaders were human and mortal, that horses were animals and not ferocious creatures or, when men were on their backs, fierce centaur-like man-beasts. They also seemed to understand Spanish combat tactics, proving adept at withstanding and reversing attacks of the conquistadors. And, if the earliest Spanish New World chroniclers are to be believed, they were led by a remarkable military strategist: Gonzalo Guerrero.

In truth, the Spanish never did conquer and fully occupy the Yucatán Peninsula. In 1546, two years after Yucatán was considered subjugated, a Mayan rebellion broke out in Valladolid and in Bacalar, a settlement established several years earlier in the southern region. Other uprisings followed, in 1639 and 1655, and in 1761 a Maya who took the ancient name of Canek led a revolt that ended in defeat and his death by torture before the public gaze in the central square of Mérida. In Canek's insurgency, though, lay the seeds of what became known as the Caste War in 1847, when the Maya were determined to drive all non-indigenous people out of the Yucatán Peninsula, and in 1848 they nearly succeeded when, having taken control of most of the peninsula, they were laying siege to and about to overwhelm Campeche and Mérida. Then suddenly recognizing that, as it had been for their ancestors for 1,000 years, it was time to plant the crops, they did a remarkable thing: they lay down their weapons and went home to cultivate their fields.

In the absence of the Mayan rebels, the ruling classes of Yucatán were able to regain control of much of the territory, but the Caste War did not officially end until fifty-six years later, in 1904. Even then resistance to outside control continued to percolate in the interior, and as late as 1933 five Maya and two soldiers were killed when the Mexican Army took control of a remote village that had never recognized federal Mexican law. And well into the twentieth century, outsiders risked their lives if they attempted to travel into some of the more remote parts of the region, encountering the kind of opposition from indigenous groups that became stronger and more formalized in the nearby southern Mexican state of Chiapas in the 1990s. There the Zapatista Army of National Liberation, largely composed of indigenous people, has fought vigorously against military and corporate control of their territory.

The Caribbean coastline from Cancún south to the city of Chetumal and the border with Belize, now the playground of so many holidayers, is not only part of this historically detached and sometimes defiant Yucatán Peninsula but also encompasses what has been for centuries the most rebellious and unmanageable region in it. The peninsula is actually composed of three states: Campeche, whose capital is the city of the same name; Yucatán, whose capital is Mérida; and Quintana Roo, whose seat of power is Chetumal. Campeche, situated in the southwestern corner, faces the Gulf of Mexico and borders Guatemala to the south and the narrow isthmus connecting it to the rest of Mexico to the south-west. Yucatán State sits to the north of it, looking across the Gulf of Mexico toward Louisiana and Texas, and, with the major cities of Mérida and Valladolid, has always dominated the region. Facing the Caribbean, Quintana Roo occupies the eastern half of the peninsula, with its border running from a point northwest of Cancún to the corner of the borders of Guatemala and Belize.

For nearly 500 years, that is, until the creation of Cancún and the development of its tourist industry, Quintana Roo has been the unruly, impenetrable, and distant sibling of Campeche and Yucatán. Without any roads to central Mexico, and lacking the coastal towns fronting the Gulf of Mexico and thus easy access to the ports of mainland Mexico, Quintana Roo was always more remote. Moreover, the southern part of the coastal territory, from Tulum to Chetumal, is largely made up of lagoons, mangrove swamps, and jungles, and this has always discouraged much exploration—or exploitation—by outsiders. It provided the safest haven for those opposed to the Spanish invasion, and its people, the descendants in spirit and perhaps in body of Guerrero, were the last to be subjugated.

While much of the Campeche and northern Yucatán regions became reasonably accessible in the 400 years after the Spanish conquest, Quintana Roo remained little known, dangerous, and difficult to reach. When American explorer and writer John L. Stephens made two historic journeys into the Yucatán Peninsula with illustrator Frederick Catherwood in 1840 and 1841, he was able to travel outside Mérida to the sites of important Mayan ruins such as Chichén Itzá, Uxmal, and Labnà. He was also able to sail to Cozumel. In order to visit Tulum, though, he had to take a boat, so he saw the site's imposing *castillo* for the first time in the same manner as Grijalva had 322 years earlier: from the sea. It was, however, as far as Catherwood and Stephens could go: as Stephens later wrote, the whole area east and south of Valladolid was "not traversed by a single road, and the rancho of Molas is the only settlement along the coast. It is a region entirely unknown; no white man ever enters it."[4]

Leap forward nearly 120 years, to 1958, and remarkably French explorer and writer Michel Peissel found Quintana Roo only a little more accessible. In order to reach it from Mexico City, he had to endure the tortuous three-day railway journey to Campeche, a bus trip to Mérida, and then another bus trip 200 miles to the northeastern, Caribbean coast. There he discovered the fictitious nature of Yucatán maps, drawn up by politicians eager to portray the region as a land of opportunity and growth and themselves as visionary builders. "Puerto Juárez," identified as lying near what is now Cancún, was not the thriving port that Peissel had expected or even a seaside village; it was composed of two small abandoned palm huts and a ten-foot-long wooden dock. Between this desolate spot and Chetumal far to the south, he reported, "lay two or three hundred miles of jungle virtually without a road."[5] Had he wanted transportation inland, Peissel would have had to take a mule-powered railway used to transport hunters and chicle collectors through thirty-eight kilometres of dense jungle from the coastal village of Puerto Morelos to Leona Vicario.[6]

The only really inhabited areas in the region were a few points around Chetumal Bay and the islands of Cozumel and Isla Mujeres. Peissel, like Stephens and Catherwood a century before, thus had to reach the coast of Quintana Roo by way of Cozumel, which he arrived at by taking a boat to Isla Mujeres and then another to Cozumel. Not following their path directly to Tulum, however, he had himself set ashore forty kilometres or so north of the famous ruins and fought his way to them on foot through the jungles, lagoons, and clouds of mosquitoes and other insects. With only the traditional Mayan houses for accommodation, the traditional food of the local population to eat, and the traditional Mayan hammock in which to sleep, Peissel got as close to the life of the indigenous people as any European outsider could in the middle of the twentieth century: "A strange feeling crept over me as for an instant I felt totally assimilated into my surroundings, to the point of wondering whether I was not a Maya. Here, lost within the jungle, lived man, and never before had I felt so close to the meaning of survival, to the meaning of life, that of primitive men of all times."[7]

When Canadian anthropologist-author Ronald Wright toured the Yucatán Peninsula in 1985, he found that in twenty-seven years Peissel's nearly deserted stretch of coastline at Puerto Juárez had become Cancún, a city of 30,000 people devoted entirely to vacationers. Tourism by then had become the third great profitable commercial enterprise in the region's history, following the production of henequen, a fibre extracted from the agave plant, in the nineteenth century and the collection of chicle in the twentieth century. Both industries collapsed as money earners when technological advances made them obsolete, leaving the economy of the Yucatán Peninsula in a state of stagnation until the Mexican government began to promote tourism there. So bustling had Cancún become, said Wright, that it was a relief to escape "south to Xaman Ha. Tourist Mexico abruptly ends; ranchitos and Maya villages reappear."[8] Thirty years later Cancún has 800,000 inhabitants, and the village that Wright called by its ancient Mayan name has become the sexier Playa del Carmen. Under its new designation, the sleepy seaside town, once known mainly as a ferry port for travellers to Cozumel, has been turned into a frenetic tourist centre, with bars, souvenir shops, malls, a Walmart store, and a Costco outlet.

Akumal, where Gonzalo Guerrero stands guard, is one of the many little coastal communities being swept along by the surge of tourism and being transformed from charming and quiet retreats into crowded and commercialized vacation spots. The seeds of that process, however, were sewn even before the conception of the Mayan Riviera. In 1958, when it was still accessible only by boat, Akumal was founded as a community for scuba divers by Mexican businessman, archaeologist, and adventurer Pablo Bush Romero. Having bought a large section of land being used as a coconut plantation, he also saw the possibilities for tourism and soon built a resort hotel; in 1972, he was able to turn the growing village into the headquarters of CEDAM (Club de Exploraciones y Deportes Acuáticos de Mexico). More recent years have seen the creation of the Centro Ecológico Akumal (CEA), an environmental organization that works to preserve the ecology of the Akumal bays and the coral reef half a kilometre offshore.

If one were looking for a perfect embodiment of the competing forces at work today in Quintana Roo's Mayan Riviera, then one could not find a better place than Akumal. Its name means "place of the turtle" in Maya, in recognition of the hawksbill, loggerhead, and green turtles that once inhabited its waters in great numbers, creatures highly valued by the ancient Maya for their eggs, flesh, and shells. Like the Maya themselves, the turtles are still there, but the beaches that for thousands of years have been the incubators of their young are now the teeming playgrounds of sun-seeking tourists, and the turtles themselves, trying to graze on the sea grass, are pursued and harassed by boatloads of snorkelling sightseers anxious to tell their friends at home that they touched an ocean turtle. Every year the CEA works assiduously to ensure that the turtles can come ashore and lay their eggs, and every year the tour operators crowd the bays with ever more invasive tourists.

Less obvious to the casual visitor to Akumal, but nonetheless alive in the background and meaningful to the local population, is the region's rich and dramatic history. As if to invoke the name of a legendary dissenter and renegade, the CEA has called its information and cultural centre, the heart of its fight to retain Akumal's centuries-old tradition, the Gonzalo Guerrero Salon. Few visitors ever discover this name or its significance, but none can miss Guerrero standing boldly in stone amid the shops, car rental stands, and restaurants, an icon who, though his true story might not ever be fully known, cannot be ignored.

The statue of Guerrero was created because of the respect of Romero for the historical foundations of Quintana Roo. In 1974, after he built his hotel and brought divers to Akumal's reefs, he wanted to celebrate the *mestizos*, the race with mixed Spanish and native American heritage so populous in and so fundamental to Mexico. He commissioned sculptor Raul Ayala to create a representation of the Yucatán Peninsula's most romantic and enigmatic figure—a Spanish castaway of the sixteenth century—and his Mayan wife and children (see frontispiece). A few years later another casting was mounted on the main beachfront avenue on Cozumel Island in a grouping called the *Monument of Two Cultures* in tribute to Guerrero's role in blending Spanish and indigenous peoples in Mexico. A third version of the Ayala sculpture stands prominently at a bustling intersection on the main avenue running into the heart of Mérida, a city that Guerrero would never have known. Towering over the major highway leading into Chetumal, a city located at the southernmost point of Quintana Roo and in the heart of the region where Guerrero would have lived among the Maya, there is a different monument created by a different sculptor.

Although somewhat romantic, the Ayala sculpture effectively represents the two most important parts of the Guerrero legend: the warrior and the father. Wearing a loincloth and sandals, adorned by large earrings, wristbands, a necklace, and an amulet, and hair done up over the forehead in Mayan style, the figure is far from the simple sailor from the shores of Castile. And no mere sailor ever looked so formidable, so extraordinarily muscular, with powerful calves and thighs that would be the envy of any modern steroidal athlete and finely chiselled arms, shoulders, and abdomen of a contemporary bodybuilder. With his resolute, heroic expression, he is every inch the warrior of his name.

But Guerrero does not stand alone; grouped around him are the other figures who embody the second, but much more important, element of the story: his place in history as the first European to marry an indigenous Mexican woman and father her children. His wife, seated gazing serenely and lovingly at him and suckling the youngest of their three children, has the common Mayan curved nose and a sturdy, substantial body. She suggests both nobility and strength. Clutching one of Guerrero's legs for protection is a naked boy looking off into the distance, and seated beside her mother is a young girl. On the ground is a Spanish conquistador's helmet, abandoned and out of place in this Mayan family tableau. Beneath this grouping is the legend "GONZALO DE GUERRERO OF PALOS DE NOGUERA, SPAIN, SEAMAN, WHO IN 1511 SHIPWRECKED NEAR THIS BEACH, MARRIED THE MAYAN PRINCESS XZAMIL AND THUS FOUNDED THE FIRST EURO-AMERICAN FAMILY."[9] The Akumal statue was originally placed on the beach so that Guerrero faced the Caribbean that had cast him up on its sands 500 years earlier, but today he stands with his back to the sea greeting the sightseers and holidayers coming in off Highway 307, the throbbing tourist artery of the peninsula. In many ways, the defiant stare, the aggressive stance, and the jutting spear are more appropriately directed toward Mérida and far beyond it to Mexico City, both seats of Spanish power that would have despised, hated, and feared him when he was alive. It was not, after all, the Maya or the Aztecs or some other indigenous people, nor was it some natural hazard of the New World, that eventually killed Guerrero. It was the Spanish themselves.

Those sixteenth-century conquistadors and chroniclers of the Spanish colonial empire could never have imagined that statues would one day be raised to Guerrero, the most reviled figure of the early days of New Spain. Despised for having married a Mayan woman and having adopted the appearance and way of life of the Maya, he was long considered a traitor by Spanish historians. He was, to sixteenth-century chroniclers, a "bad Christian," a "traitor and apostate sailor," and an "infidel mariner." Given the opportunity to rejoin his countrymen after seven years in the jungle and assist Cortés in conquering the Aztecs, he chose to remain a "savage." Worse yet, he was seen as being responsible for the long and difficult struggle to subdue the natives of the Yucatán Peninsula, a shrewd tactician who taught the Maya that the Spanish were not gods but men who could be beaten by those who knew their battle strategies and their weaknesses. Behind every defeat of the conquistadors, behind every failure to subdue another rebellious native tribe, the chroniclers saw the treasonous hand of Guerrero.

Even today there are those in central Mexico who blame Guerrero for delaying the Spanish conquest of the Yucatán Peninsula and what they see as the healthy assimilation of the Maya into the Spanish dominion. In Quintana Roo and throughout the peninsula, however, he is now celebrated as one of its most heroic and beloved figures. He is the father of the first children ever born of the union between a European and an indigenous Mexican; the symbolic father of the *mestizo* race (i.e., 60 per cent of modern Mexicans); the first man who, in his own family, united the two rich traditions and heritages that make up modern Mexico, two civilizations that had existed for thousands of years oblivious of each other: Spain and America. More than that, Guerrero has come to embody the spirit of the peninsula, the determination to fight assimilation by the rest of the country, to remain La Hermana República de Mexico, "the Sister Republic of Mexico," rather than just another region. That is a colossal weight for one man to bear, a role in history beyond anything that a humble sailor from a coastal village in Spain could have imagined for himself. But the life of Gonzalo Guerrero, from its origins in fifteenth-century rural Andalusia to its sensational end in the jungle of Central America, has become one of Mexico's most fascinating legends.

CHAPTER TWO

"To Serve God and ... to Get Rich":
THE LURE OF THE NEW WORLD

he salt air of adventure which blew about Moguer might well have infected any young man of spirit."[1] Kathleen Romoli, the biographer of Vasco Núñez de Balboa, was describing one community along Spain's Atlantic southern coast, but she could just as well have been referring to a host of towns and villages. Walk through any of the streets of Palos de la Frontera, Huelva, Lepe, Mazagón, or Sanlúcar de Barrameda, and it is impossible to forget that it was from them that the monumental voyages of exploration of the late fifteenth and early sixteenth centuries were launched. Christopher Columbus set off in his little fleet from Palos, a short way inland on the Rio Tinto, to reach the Far East and instead found a whole new continent. Balboa, who became the first European to see the Pacific Ocean from America, left from Moguer, seven kilometres farther upriver, and Hernán Cortés, the great conquistador who captured Montezuma's immense Aztec

Empire, sailed from Sanlúcar de Barrameda, down the coast. It was from Sanlúcar, too, that Ferdinand Magellan set out to circumnavigate the globe, a journey that he did not live to complete but one that saw him lead the first ships to sail from the Atlantic into the Pacific and across that vast ocean. Not for nothing does Palos call itself "the cradle of the Discovery of the New World."

In various chronicles and histories, Gonzalo Guerrero is described as having come from Moguer, Lepe, Niebla, or Huelva, but most often he is said to have been born, raised, and trained as a sailor in Palos. In the end, it matters little which of these towns was his birthplace; all are clustered in the southern region of Spain known as Andalusia, the part of Castile that was the conduit through which the overseas explorers and empire builders passed on their way to the New World, to Africa, and to the Far East. As such, there could have been no better place or time in Spanish history for a young man to come to maturity.

It is likely that Gonzalo was in his early twenties when he sailed to the New World around 1509, two years before his arrival in Mexico. In the years around his departure, Spain acquired the largest overseas empire in the world and became the most powerful and wealthy country in Europe. For a young man with ambition, energy, and a spirit of adventure, the world offered possibilities as never before. In the words of one historian, "to be young in the Hispanic Peninsula during this period of human experience was to have faith in the impossible. An enormously enlarged world teemed with possibilities of adventure, riches, and romance in which the wildest dreams and the fondest hopes of fame and fortune might be fulfilled."[2]

For someone so revered on the Yucatán Peninsula, very little is known about Guerrero before he clambered onto its shore in 1512. His origins remain as elusive and enigmatic to historians as he himself was a mystery to the conquistadors who later hunted him in the Yucatán jungles, and this is largely because his real name was long ago lost and replaced by a legendary one. He became known variously as Gonzalo Marinero (i.e., "sailor"), Gonzalo de Aroça, and Gonzalo de Aroza, designations that are of little use, being labels denoting occupation or background rather than true names. Guerrero, the name by which he is known everywhere in Mexico today, and which means "warrior" or "martial, warlike" in Spanish, is an appellation invented by chroniclers to fit the legend of a military genius.

As a boy and an adolescent in Andalusia, Gonzalo would have witnessed remarkable changes to life around him and to the society emerging in what would become Spain. For more than 2,000 years of settlement by a series of colonizers—Phoenicians, Greeks, Carthaginians, Romans, and Moors—the shores of the Atlantic Ocean, called the Ocean Sea, were the farthest reach of empire. There was a good reason for Palos—and numerous other Andalusian towns and villages—being called de la Frontera ("of the Frontier"); they were the frontier beyond which it was impossible to go. The vast land mass of Eurasia, stretching from Siberia and China in the East, ended at the Spanish-Portuguese coast. Beyond that lay the forbidding body of water also known as the Mare Ignotum, the "Sea of Mystery."

If, as a young boy, Gonzalo was taken the few kilometres to the seaside, then he would have looked out at a vast ocean that was not only the object of mystery but also the source of dread. Its depths were said to be the haunts of all manner of horrific sea serpents, and its islands were reputed to be homes to strange creatures: hairy giants and wild men, Cyclops, dog-headed people, Amazons who could enslave men, and sirens and mermaids who would entice sailors to their deaths. In one of the Greek myths, the mighty Hercules narrowed the Strait of Gibraltar to prevent such monsters from invading the Mediterranean from the Atlantic. The Pillars of Hercules, which legend said he planted on either side of the strait, were said to bear the inscription *Non Plus Ultra* ("Nothing Farther Beyond") as a warning to sailors to go no farther.

Such myths and wild speculations are inevitable human responses to the unknown, and for centuries they troubled uneducated and superstitious seamen along the Atlantic coast. There was, however, a much more practical reason for a lack of exploration of the farther reaches of the Ocean Sea: the trade winds. Those of the North Atlantic are westerly, meaning that any ship heading out into the ocean had to fight strong headwinds. Because it was almost impossible to make any westward progress, the Portuguese discovery of the Azores in 1431 marked the first time in history that humans had ever set foot on the islands.

The men of Gonzalo's town did go to sea, of course, but they remained in coastal waters to fish and trade up and down the Iberian coast. Occasionally, they ranged much farther, travelling across the Strait of Gibraltar and down the west coast of Africa to Guinea in search of slaves and valuable minerals. By the end of the fifteenth century, Palos and the surrounding towns had become renowned for their skilled, knowledgeable, and experienced sailors, and it was inevitable that this region of Spain would provide most of the navigators and explorers of the New World.

Ironically, the trade winds that caused the Atlantic to be an impassable boundary for 2,000 years also made the Iberian Peninsula the most favourable place in Europe from which to launch a search for new and exotic lands. The winds of the Atlantic follow a clockwise pattern: south from Spain, west from Africa to the Caribbean, northeast up the American coast, and east across the Atlantic to the northern European coast. With enough imagination, courage, and confidence, it was possible to use the easterlies off the coast of Africa to sail across the ocean and then catch the westerlies and be taken back across to the Azores and Portugal. No one with these qualities—some would say foolhardiness—was prepared to attempt such a voyage until the Genoese navigator, Christopher Columbus, arrived in Palos from Portugal in 1485. Lodged and fed by the friars of the nearby Monastery of la Rábida, men whose lives close to the sea made them knowledgeable and sympathetic allies, he spent months devising a plan to persuade the Spanish monarchs, Isabella of Castile and Ferdinand of Aragon, to invest in his scheme to sail west across the Ocean Sea in search of the spice- and jewel-rich Indies: that is, India, China, and Japan.

Columbus's appearance in Palos must have nearly coincided with Gonzalo's birth, but the boy was at least seven years old before he saw any sign of the great navigator's expedition. Columbus had failed to convince the king of Portugal to support his plan, his brother Bartholomew had no more success in England and France, and until 1492 his periodic hearings produced nothing in the Spanish court. Then suddenly and dramatically in January of that remarkable year the Spanish monarchs decided to sponsor his Enterprise of the Indies, as he called his venture.

The hesitation of Isabella and Ferdinand to support Columbus might have reflected widespread skepticism about his project, but they were also preoccupied with making profound changes to their country. At the same time, these changes led the monarchs to see the value in Atlantic exploration and ultimately led to the great Spanish overseas empire of the sixteenth century. They were transformations that not only altered the society in which Guerrero grew up but also shaped the attitudes of young men like him as they set out for the New World. In his case, they were attitudes that would be deeply challenged by what he would find on the Yucatán Peninsula.

At the time of Guerrero's birth, Spain as it is known today—that is, a unified country occupying much of the Iberian Peninsula—had just come into being. Having been divided for centuries into a number of Christian kingdoms at war with Moorish invaders who had crossed the Mediterranean in 711 CE, the area became united by the marriage of Isabella, who had become Queen of Castile in 1474, and Ferdinand, who succeeded to the throne of Aragon in 1479. Although their marriage seems to have been an alliance of equals, Castile, of which Andalusia was a vital region, was the larger, more vigorous, and dominant partner, and it was this part of Spain that bred the conquistadors and empire builders.

As Spain began to take shape as a unified and powerful entity, Ferdinand and Isabella were pressed to conquer the last remaining area of the peninsula under Moorish control, the Emirate of Granada, and thus eliminate a Muslim enclave that might undermine Catholic Spain. It took a decade of battles, but, as the story goes, on January 2, 1492, Granada's ruler, Boabdil, knelt before Ferdinand and tearfully surrendered the keys to the city, an action that prompted his formidable mother to say contemptuously, "You do well to weep like a woman for what you could not defend like a man."[3] When news of the defeat of the Moors was made public in early February, there was great jubilation in Italy and Spain. In Rome, the pope celebrated a special mass in the Church of Saint James the Great, the patron saint of Spain, and he conferred on Ferdinand and Isabella the title of Reyes Católicos, the "Catholic Kings." In Spain, one observer described the fall of Granada as "the most distinguished and blessed day there has ever dawned in Spain," and the historian of the Spanish court, Peter Martyr of Anghiera, called it "the extinction of Spain's calamities."[4]

The Muslim presence had given Iberia a cultural and intellectual richness, but it was seen as a Christian victory, celebrated by the court of Isabella and Ferdinand in numerous ceremonies and drawing congratulatory letters from various European monarchs. If the joyous news was also observed by festivities in the towns and villages throughout Castile, particularly in the southern regions adjoining Granada, then Gonzalo would have been aware that something important had changed in his world.

It was a change that ultimately went far beyond mere political control to a profound transformation of the Spanish character. For nearly eight centuries, Muslims had been part of the fabric of Castilian life, especially in the south—the name Andalusia was derived in fact from the Muslim label for the territory, al-Andalus—and, while attempting to limit the power of Muslims,

Christians had tolerated them. This was a pragmatic accommodation that, when it included the sizable Jewish population, came to be known by Spanish historians as the time of the *convivencia*: that is, "living together." As a result, much of Spanish architecture, art, and culture was influenced by the three religions to a degree not seen elsewhere in Europe.

The fall of Granada signalled the end of the *convivencia* and its replacement by religious and ethnic cleansing on a massive scale, a program that ultimately inspired the Spanish search for overseas converts and an extensive Catholic empire. The defeat of the Moors had drawn praise from all corners of Europe for its expansion of Christian power and influence, and Ferdinand and Isabella became imbued with the idea of being, as Pope Innocent VIII proclaimed them, "athletes of Christ." Within three months, they took two steps to purify their country of heretics and spread the one true faith—Catholicism—throughout the world, a world on the verge of becoming enlarged beyond anyone's imagination.

For fourteen years, Ferdinand and Isabella had conducted a campaign against *conversos*, Jews who had "converted" to Christianity and thereby become prominent members of Spanish society: bankers, court secretaries, and even priors and bishops. The Inquisition had been created in 1478 to exterminate any *conversos* suspected of continuing secretly to practise their religion, and over the years several thousand people were subjected to rigged trials, torture, forced confessions, and finally burning at the stake.

In the exhilaration following the defeat of Granada, when the country seemed to be expunging one influential religion, the Catholic kings seem to have concluded that it was time to drive out another. Thus, on April 29, 1492, they issued a decree requiring Jews to convert to Catholicism; those who would not become Christians were given three months to sell their properties and effects and leave the country.

Somewhere between 100,000 and 200,000 Jews chose exile, and, like all such hurried and forced exoduses, their leaving was chaotic, miserable, and marked by death on a large scale. All over Castile, groups of Jews made their ways as best they could to the nearest seaport. "They went by the roads and fields with great labour and misery," reported one chronicler, "some falling, some struggling again to their feet, others dying or falling sick." On sighting the sea, "they uttered loud screams and wailing, men and women, old and young, begging for God's mercy, for they hoped for some miracle from God and that the sea would part to make a road for them....Many wished they had never been born."[5] Numerous Jews who did secure passage out of Castile were charged exorbitant fees, and some were then thrown overboard at sea. Others who were rumoured to have swallowed gold and diamonds as a means of smuggling their wealth out of the country were killed and cut open for the suspected treasure.

The young Gonzalo would certainly have witnessed some of this wretched spectacle; few villages and towns in Andalusia did not behold suffering on a large scale. Their streets were crowded and noisy with desperate refugees seeking ships to take them to North Africa, Italy, or the Middle East. Even a Christian chronicler hostile to the Jews wrote that "there was not a Christian who did not feel their pain."[6]

At the same time as this expulsion was occurring, Gonzalo would have seen the other momentous consequence of the fall of Granada: the authorizing of Columbus to attempt to sail to the Indies. On January 6, 1492, the navigator had been part of the exultant procession that accompanied Ferdinand and Isabella as they entered Granada to the sounds of trumpets and drums and the raising of royal standards above the city. Columbus was there to press his case to a court that had rejected his earlier bids, and this time the monarchs eagerly agreed to his proposal. Their change of heart was the result of being persuaded that, having just done great service to Christianity and God with the defeat of the Moors, they could do so much more if, in their names, this Genoese navigator found new lands and new converts to the one true faith. Spain was being swept by a fervent belief that its destiny was to spread Catholicism over vast areas of the world, and Columbus might be the instrument to realize it.

Columbus himself later wrote that the fall of Granada had been a catalyst for his voyages because it convinced the Spanish monarchs that they could conquer other parts of the world and convert their inhabitants: Ferdinand and Isabella, "as enemies of the Muslim sect and of all idolatries and heresies, ordered that I should go to the east." He also linked his commission with the expulsion of the Jews, noting in his diary that, "after having banished all the Jews from all your Kingdoms and realms,... Your Highnesses ordered me to go with a sufficient fleet to the said regions of India."[7]

Columbus's choice of Palos as the port from which his expedition would depart was influenced at least in part by the upheaval of the Jewish emigration. Cadiz, being much larger, would have been more suitable, but it had been designated as an embarkation point for Jews, and, clogged with throngs of miserable and desperate refugees, it would have been difficult to outfit ships and find crews. Even in Palos, Columbus had to schedule his departure so as to avoid the confusion, so he left on August 3, the day immediately following the deadline for all unconverted Jews to leave Spain. Despite this delay, an old Spaniard later swore that, as a boy, he watched Columbus's fleet move out of the port while he was standing on the deck of a ship riding dangerously low in the water from being overloaded with fleeing Jews.[8]

There were several other reasons why Columbus chose Palos. First, it was close to the Monastery of la Rábida, where he and his six-year-old son, Diego, had been taken in, lodged, and fed on their arrival from Portugal in 1485. More than merely providing physical support and comfort, the friars had lifted the spirits of the discouraged navigator with their knowledge of the sea, their encouragement, and their connections to influential figures. Second, the men of Palos and the surrounding towns were renowned for their hardy seamanship and likely to provide the crews needed to take the little ships to the Indies and back. Third and most importantly, Palos could provide important material support for the expedition.

Columbus arrived at the port on May 22, and the next day the town's mayor and councillors were given a letter that he brought from Ferdinand and Isabella informing them that, for certain unnamed things that they had done to "the disservice" of the royal court, they were required to provide two caravels (small, light, speedy ships under 100 tons). These craft were to be ready in ten days and available to Columbus for one year. In fact, it took seventy-two days for the *Pinta* and *Niña* to be fitted out and for crews to be hired.

If Gonzalo was as inquisitive as most young boys, then he would have been well aware of the bustle of activity in the harbour at Palos in the summer of 1492. And if he paid attention to the conversations of the men of the town, then he would undoubtedly have heard some of their bitter grumbling about the costs to the community of Columbus's venture. In addition to its demand for two caravels, the royal court commanded that various carpenters, timber merchants, ship chandlers, bakers, winemakers, and other provision dealers furnish Columbus with what he needed at reasonable prices, free of any customs or excises against any of the materials or provisions. Royal patronage on this scale—and the palpable resentment that it produced in the townspeople—would not have gone unnoticed even by local youth.

Gonzalo might well have picked up snatches of gossip about young local sailors, and those of Huelva, Moguer, and other coastal towns, enlisting with the Genoese captain on a risky, far-fetched, and dangerous voyage. They might have been knowledgeable and experienced, and hardened to the sea by voyages along the West African coast, but setting out across the Ocean Sea beyond the known outposts of the Azores and Canary Islands, however, was a much different matter. It was a voyage into the unknown, and Palos might never again see many of its husbands, sons, and brothers.

A sign of the reluctance of Andalusian sailors to join such a risky venture was the edict from Isabella and Ferdinand that anybody held on civil and criminal prosecutions would be pardoned if they signed up for the venture. Four or five such lawbreakers, one of whom had actually killed a man in a fight, did sail with the fleet. In addition, at least one Jew managed to enlist, as did a *converso*, whose knowledge of Hebrew and Arabic would enable him to translate conversations with the Far Eastern courts.

Drawing on a variety of sources, Columbus was able to assemble a crew of about ninety men, and, with the addition of a larger third ship, the *Santa María*, his little fleet slipped out of the harbour in Palos half an hour before dawn on August 3. Among the last tasks to be completed were filling the casks with a year's supply of fresh water from the fountain at the Church of Saint George and ensuring that every member of the crew confessed his sins, received absolution, and took communion. That done, Columbus ordered the ships to be blessed, the sails to be set in the name of Jesus Christ, and the ensigns of the Holy Cross and of Ferdinand and Isabella raised. With the sailors' wives and other townspeople waving farewell, the craft left Palos and, carried on a windless day by the current of the Rio Tinto, disappeared out to sea.

Columbus was undoubtedly excited to be on his way at last, and Palos was likely glad to see the end of him, at least for some time. How much of a stir was created in the town by a small fleet leaving with such ceremony and flying the royal ensigns, and whether a boy named Gonzalo was there to see it, we can only imagine. But, if he lived in Palos, he could not have missed the excitement and colour of the navigator's return 224 days later. Columbus had already landed by then in the Azores and then in Portugal, where he had repaired the *Niña* and sent letters to the Spanish court informing it of his discoveries and his return. Then, on Friday, March 15, to the astonishment and delight of the voyagers' relatives and friends, many of whom had long given them up for lost, the *Niña*, closely followed by the *Pinta*, sailed into the harbour at

Palos. The *Santa María* had run aground earlier and been abandoned off the coast of Española, but the sight of the remaining two ships, in the words of one historian, set off a wild celebration:

> A crowd stared at the tiny caravel in disbelief as it anchored. Then, as if in one massive reflex, the flock of men rushed toward the *Niña*.
>
> Once the news spread about Columbus's discovery, the citizens of Palos thronged to the caravel. Mesmerized by the Indians, the strange plants, birds, and foods from the Indies and by the sailors' stories, the enraptured citizenry followed Columbus to church for thanksgiving service. To announce the historic landing, all the church bells of Palos were rung. In the ensuing confusion Columbus and his crewmen were carried through the streets and caught up in a dizzying round of *bodas y banquetes*, celebrations and festivities.[9]

Perhaps only important officials and townspeople were permitted to view the collection of exotic specimens that Columbus brought back with him: parrots and other colourful birds, *hutias* (large Caribbean rodents), monkeys, sweet potatoes, chili peppers, and a small quantity of gold. Curious bystanders watching the procession going through the streets of Palos, though, would have craned their necks to see six strange people walking with the Spaniards. They were Tainos, snatched as slaves from Caribbean islands, men described as having complexions "the colour of quince jelly" and wearing garments exotic to Andalusian eyes.[10] Adding to the fascination were their gold earrings and nostril rings, a custom that would become fashionable in the Western world 500 years later but was considered barbaric to fifteenth-century Europeans. A custom, moreover, that Gonzalo himself would embrace years later in the New World.

Columbus left Palos in triumph, and no one, not even a young Gonzalo, could have been unmoved by the excitement of his progress toward the royal court in Barcelona. Passing through Seville, he was cheered by spectators in windows, on balconies, and on rooftops, and along the roads his progress was slowed by those who wanted a view of the great navigator. Then, before Ferdinand and Isabella and the Spanish nobility, he gave an account of his discoveries. Nothing would ever be the same for their world or for the New World, and nothing would ever be the same for Andalusia and young men like Gonzalo.

So sensational was the discovery by Columbus that nineteen editions of his famous *Letter on His First Voyage*, intended to be a public statement of his voyage, were published between 1493 and 1500. Although Columbus continued to maintain that he had reached the Indies—a claim finally discredited in 1503 when Amerigo Vespucci's pamphlet *Mundus Novus* argued instead that he had found an entirely new continent—the Spanish wanted to secure their right to his discoveries. Pope Alexander VI took out a map of the world, drew a line from pole to pole 100 leagues west of the Azores, and stated imperiously in three papal bulls that everything east of the line would belong to Portugal, while everything west of it would belong to the monarchs of Spain and their successors forever. This astonishing division of the world between the two Catholic countries, which they ratified a year later with the Treaty of Tordesillas, naturally appalled the rest of Europe. For the Spanish, however, it was further confirmation of their destiny to conquer and convert the world to Catholicism, and they began to pursue it with even greater zeal.

While the Spanish were eager to take their one true faith to the rest of the world, they were as fervent in bringing back its riches. Columbus cleverly managed to tie the plundering of the New World with the spread of Catholicism in a letter to Ferdinand and Isabella in 1503: "Gold is most excellent. Gold is treasure, and with it, whoever has it may do what he wants in the world, and may succeed in taking souls to Paradise." Years later a companion of Hernán Cortés and the chronicler of his conquest of Mexico said more candidly that "we came here to serve God and the king, and also to get rich."[11]

The lust for overseas treasure had been sparked in the Spanish imagination long before, and it had now been fanned into flame by the discovery of the Indies. For centuries, there had been folktales and highly fantastic printed accounts of incredible wealth to be found on islands far out into the Atlantic: cities of gold, rivers in which pearls were as abundant as pebbles, fountains and lakes of gigantic jewels. Those riches, so it was said, were there simply to be scooped up by enterprising explorers. These fanciful tales were given some credibility when Columbus and subsequent adventurers began to return with exotic cargo and intriguing stories. Although the great sources of gold would not be found until the defeat of the Aztecs in Mexico and the Inca in Peru, Columbus was able to show some gold that he had acquired in the Caribbean islands. And in 1500, as if to prove the folktales correct, a young sailor from Moguer, Peralonso Niño, came back from a small expedition to the New World with a visible hoard of fifty pounds of pearls and widespread rumours of much more that he had smuggled to avoid giving the crown its share.

Even when travellers returned with disappointing amounts of treasure, they usually brought tales of gold and precious gems that could be found with more widespread exploration. Financial backers of expeditions needed reassurances about their investments, and thus gold is everywhere in Columbus's account of his first voyage. In this inflated reporting, explorers were aided by natives of the Caribbean islands, who, quickly becoming sensitive to Spaniards' obsession with gold and pearls, learned that elaborately fabricated descriptions of unlimited riches on the next island or in the land over the mountain range would often rid them of the intruders. Such stories found their way back to Spain and became common currency on the streets, in the homes, and on the docks of its coastal towns.

Who were the men captivated by the promise of New World riches? They were, in fact, all sorts: minor aristocrats, middle-class merchants and entrepreneurs, working-class labourers, and soldiers of fortune. The leaders of expeditions most often were younger sons of noble families forced to seek land, wealth, and prestige abroad. The followers were middle- and lower-class men for whom the Indies offered the timeless appeal to emigrants: a much better life than they had or could achieve in their homeland.

Castile had endured four widespread famines in the fifteenth century—leading to the Spanish proverb that, "if the lark flies over Castile, she must take her grain of barley with her"[12] —and life in Andalusia had always been particularly difficult. Eleven famines there meant thirty-five years of food shortages, starvation, and social unrest. A series of harvest failures in the early years of the sixteenth century, when Gonzalo was approaching young manhood, made economic conditions especially grim.

Ironically, while the discovery of the New World and the subsequent rush of men to go there initially benefited the coastal towns of Andalusia, the same catalyst for trading activity eventually led to a decline in the fortunes of Palos. A town of around 2,500 people when Gonzalo was born, it shrank dramatically when he was a young man because so many of its people left for the Indies or Seville, which had become the busy centre of the Atlantic trade. Any young man with ambition could be forgiven for thinking that he would miss his great opportunity if he did not join those boarding the ships.

If Gonzalo came from a family of seamen, then a successful venture in the New World could offer something perhaps as important as wealth: escape from a life narrowly circumscribed by class restrictions. In Spain, a young man could rise—and then only modestly—from a humble background through two means: the church and the military. In the Indies, however, a Spanish workman could become a landowner and the master of a number of indigenous slaves. If his venture was successful, then he might eventually return a rich man to his homeland, where social distinction was measured by land and wealth. So attractive was this possibility of social mobility and independence from class restrictions that in

1518 a seventy-year-old man tried to emigrate. "You, father," he was asked, "why do you want to go to the Indies, being so old and tired?" He replied, "By my faith, sir, to die and leave my sons in a free and happy land."[13]

To this heady cocktail of religious zeal, wealth, and social mobility must be added one more intoxicating ingredient of sixteenth-century Spanish life: the ideals of chivalric romance. For centuries, the feats of mythical and historical heroes—El Cid, Alexander the Great, Charlemagne, Hannibal, and countless lesser figures—had fired the imaginations of Castilians in ballads and poems. The introduction of printing to Spain in 1473 meant that many of the conquistadors and adventurers of what Hugh Thomas calls "the generation of 1500"—that is, Guerrero's generation—were possibly able to read about, or at least hear oral renditions of, such exploits. Moreover, new legendary figures appeared in a series of fictional romances, the most famous of which was *Amadís de Gaula*, written two centuries earlier but first published in 1508.

Like the superheroes of twentieth-century comic books and films, the hero of *Amadís de Gaula* offered the young men of Spain a model of invincible yet gentle knighthood. Called The Knight of the Green Sword, Amadís is courteous, sensitive, and Christian, but he is also a fierce warrior who kills countless opponents in battle. He wins the hand of the daughter of a king, but in order to prove himself he travels the world rescuing the unfortunate, fighting duels, capturing lands, and killing monsters such as the scaly giant Endriago, who exhales a noxious stench.

Amadís de Gaula and its many imitators were brilliantly parodied a century after their publication by Miguel de Cervantes in *Don Quixote*, but there is no doubt that such romances, in ballad and written forms, were in the minds of explorers of the New World as they sought an empire for Spain and fame for themselves. Among the 100 books leaving Sanlúcar for the Indies in 1505 were thirty-four romances, and, on first seeing the marvellous Aztec city of Tenochtitlán, Bernal Díaz del Castillo reported that "it was like the enchantments they tell of in the legend of Amadis, on account of the great towers and cues and buildings rising from the water."[14] So much did the tales of chivalry and adventure travel with the empire builders that they often gave mythical names to their discoveries. California came from a fictional sequel to *Amadís de Gaula*, Patagonia from *Primaleon* (1512), Amazon River from the ancient Greek myth, and Antilles from the myth of Atlantis. Similarly, Italian explorer Giovanni da Verrazzano used a name from ancient Greek mythology, Arcadia, to identify the North American coastal region in his 1548 map.

The role of chivalric ideals in motivating the Spanish explorations of the sixteenth century was significant, but historian Felipe Fernández-Armesto goes further in arguing that they were unique to all of Renaissance Europe and lay behind its great empire building. There was, he writes, "only one feature that did make the region peculiarly conducive to breeding explorers. They were steeped in the idealization of adventure. Many of them shared or strove to embody the great aristocratic ethos of their day—the 'code' of chivalry. Their ships were gaily caparisoned steeds, and they rode the waves like jennets."[15]

Young manhood was shaped for Guerrero by a period of great passion for overseas exploration, and he lived in the part of the world most affected by that passion. No region of Spain—or indeed of Europe—had been as caught up in the rush to follow Columbus's daring and to exploit the possibilities of the New World as the Andalusian coast. Cadiz became a key port when Columbus launched his second voyage from it in October 1493, an expedition of seventeen vessels and 1,500 workmen and artisans. Seville, seventy kilometres up the broad Rio Guadalquivir from the coast, became one of the great commercial centres of Europe by being given, in 1503, absolute control over all trade between Spain and its emerging empire. An estimated 200 ships left from Andalusian ports between 1506 and 1518, and many of them carried men from the smaller towns and villages, such as Palos and Moguer. One of them was Guerrero.

There is no record of the date that he sailed for the New World or of the name of his vessel, but, since he is known to have been in Darién, the first Spanish settlement on the American mainland, in 1510, he was likely part of the fleet of eight or nine ships that sailed to the region from Sanlúcar in September 1509. Located on land on the Isthmus of Panama first discovered in 1501, a colony there had been expected for some years to become a vital centre for harvesting gold and valuable gems reputed to lie in abundance in the nearby mountains. The death of Queen Isabella in 1504, however, and the subsequent struggle over succession to the Spanish crown, meant that little attention was paid to any expansion of an empire in the Indies until 1508. Development of the mainland settlement stagnated until two competing entrepreneurs, Diego de Nicuesa and Alonso de Hojeda, were given official permission to explore and settle large parcels of land stretching from the north coast of present-day Colombia up to, and including, the Isthmus of Panama. Thus in 1509 a new wave of settlers was dispatched in a flotilla that carried 200 passengers from Spain and 600 more who were already established landowners on the island of Hispaniola.

When the promoters of this new colonial enterprise cast their nets along the Andalusian coast for adventurous souls to explore the New World, they caught the imagination of a young Gonzalo. If he had sailed as one of the potential settlers, his passage would have cost him eleven ducats, the equivalent of a year's wages for an unskilled workman in Spain. As a member of a ship's crew, the only position open to a young man from a humble Palos background, he was able to work his way across the Atlantic.

In either case, one can envisage Gonzalo watching his native shores along Sanlúcar recede into the distance, perhaps wondering when, if ever, he would next see them and his family and home. Turning his face to the wide Atlantic horizon and the six-week voyage to the New World, what must he have thought lay ahead? What encounters, what experiences, what dangers, and what triumphs would await him, and how might they change his life? He went armed with the certainty that Spain was destined to rule the lands of riches and opportunities that Columbus had discovered—had not God, through Pope Alexander VI, decreed it so? He was leaving a newly emerged country that had expunged the other by expelling Muslims and Jews to leave the one true religion, Catholicism, triumphant throughout the land. That triumph would be repeated wherever the Spanish encountered savages and pagans until the world was won for the "athletes of Christ." Like a figure from the chivalric romances, Gonzalo would be part of that crusade. And he might return from it a rich and respected man.

He could not have imagined how the New World would shatter these attitudes and transform him utterly.

CHAPTER THREE

"It Seemed the End of the World":
BALBOA, PIZARRO, AND THE PERILS OF DARIÉN

When Gonzalo Guerrero set out across the Ocean Sea, he was not, like the crewmen of the *Niña*, *Pinta*, and *Santa María* before him, facing the unknown. In the seventeen years since Columbus had broken through the invisible but formidable barrier of the "Sea of Mystery," hundreds of ships had sailed from the Andalusian coast to the Spanish Indies. A base had been established on what Columbus had named La Ysla Española (later called Hispaniola), the Caribbean island that today comprises the countries of Haiti and the Dominican Republic. From there, the Spanish had begun to map the coastlines of the adjoining islands and to understand the currents, shoals, and weather patterns of the Caribbean Sea. Each vessel that returned to Cadiz or Sanlúcar de Barrameda brought with it seamen increasingly experienced in dealing with the hazards of Atlantic crossings.

Travel to and from the New World was nonetheless still perilous. Navigation was conducted by sighting the stars, and it involved more guesswork and prayer than science. Spanish seamen had the cross-staff and astrolabe, but the latter, then still in its early form, was almost useless on the heaving deck of a ship or on a vessel tacking across strong winds. The ships themselves were small craft on which to face an open sea notorious for its unpredictable and sudden violent storms. The caravel, which had taken Columbus to the New World, had begun to be replaced by the slightly heavier, three-masted *nao* (or carrick), but it too was not much larger than twenty-first-century yachts. Without the engines that power the modern craft, the ship that carried Gonzalo was prey both to the doldrums that halted progress and to the fierce gales that could blow a vessel hundreds of miles off course.

The sea extinguished the hopes—and the lives—of many adventurous souls pursuing dreams of a better life. Columbus himself had lost the *Santa María* when it ran aground off Española on Christmas Day in 1492. On a voyage six years later, some of his ships lost their course and had their cargoes spoiled. In 1502, twenty-seven ships left Sanlúcar, but before they had reached even the Canary Islands they were beset by a raging storm that sank one of them with 120 persons aboard, forced others to jettison their cargoes, and scattered the fleet. In July of the same year, a fleet of twenty-three craft returning to Spain from Española encountered a storm so fierce that Columbus himself, seemingly anchored safely in harbour, wrote that "my ships practically fell apart. Each ship pulled at its anchor without hope, except for death."[1] All but three of the vessels sank, with a grievous loss of life and cargo, and ultimately only one of the ships reached Spain.

Less serious than the mortal dangers of fifteenth-century sea travel, but hardly less formidable, were the sheer discomforts of a voyage. Gonzalo would have been accustomed to the rough life of a sailor plying his trade off the Andalusian coast and along the North African shores, but a six- to eight-week crossing of the Ocean Sea was a far different matter. On such long passages, the small ships became islands of stifling claustrophobia moving over a seascape of unbroken monotony. Little wonder, then, if Gonzalo, on the steady legs of an experienced seaman, occasionally joined his mates in their pastime of watching the heaving of seasick land-lubbers who had paid for their passage.

One such passenger, Eugenio de Salazar, left a vivid picture of a similar voyage made later in the sixteenth century. The ship, he said, was "what some call a rack for criminals, others a wooden hack-horse, and others a pig-bird.... There are rooms so closed, dark, and smelly that they seem like charnel houses of the dead...like the wombs of hell." Since the caulking of the time could never ensure watertight vessels, seawater regularly leaked into the bilge at the bottom of the hold, and to this water was regularly added garbage and other waste. Despite the operation of hand-driven pumps, no one aboard could be unaware of the bilge's "flowing rivers, not of sweet-running crystal waters, but of curdy nastiness; not filled with grains of gold...but with vulgar, misshapen pearls from the toilets, and of lice."[2] Less numerous than the lice but more apparent to the eyes were the ever-present cockroaches and rats.

In one respect, the passengers had a more comfortable crossing than crewmen like Gonzalo. On his first voyage, Columbus had discovered the native islanders, the Tainos, sleeping in hammocks, a practice unknown in Europe but common all over Central America, and it was quickly adopted for paying customers aboard ships. Regular sailors, however, slept wherever they could find an unoccupied floor space—on deck in fair weather and below in foul—using a coil of heavy rope or sail as a pillow and a brace against the pitching and rolling of the vessel.

Passengers from comfortable backgrounds would have found the ship's food a step down from what they were accustomed to, but the crew ate as well as their working counterparts back in Castile. Everyone, though, quickly tired of the repetitious menu. Breakfast for seamen on the early watch consisted of a ship's biscuit or hardtack, baked on land and, if the crew were lucky, kept dry and relatively free of maggots at sea. To this was added some garlic, cheese, and salted sardines or anchovies, washed down with water or wine, the only beverages carried aboard Spanish ships of the time. The one hot meal of the day was served at 11 a.m. and could include salted meat or fish, fresh fish if the waters were generous, chickpeas, lentils, beans, rice, honey, and almonds. The cooking was done on an open firebox, so dangerous in rough weather that dinners were often eaten cold. Indeed, such was the fear of fire breaking out aboard the wooden vessels that the only nighttime illumination came from a helmsman's light at the stern.

Nothing is known of Gonzalo's role as a crewman. If Gonzalo were very young, he would have been a *gromet*, or "ship's boy," whose main duty was to watch and turn the fragile glass *ampolleta*, a half-hour "sand clock" that was the only way of telling time at sea. Pages, like *gromets*, served the regular seamen, swept up, washed dishes, and said prayers. A keeper of the arms and storeroom steward managed the provisions, a boatswain supervised the loading and storing of cargo, a caulker tried to keep the ship reasonably watertight, a cooper kept the water and wine casks intact, a carpenter saw to repairs, and a barber-doctor cut hair and let blood if necessary. All of these crewmen took orders from a chain of command headed by the pilot, captain, and master.

If, as is likely, Gonzalo was a *marinero*, an able "seaman," he served his watches in a variety of duties: overhauling gear, making and setting sails, working bilge pumps, trimming sheets, scrubbing rails, and washing and clearing decks with stiff brooms made of twigs. Other activities, dictated by the orders of the pilot, were more vigorous and risky. "You will see," wrote Salazar, "some [sailors] in the maintopsail yards, others climbing shrouds. Still other gentlemen are in the lateen [sail] yards, or hugging the masthead. Others are glued to the mast steps or hauling sheets. Others climb about the rigging, some high, some low, like cats in trees, or spirits that fell from heaven and remained in the air."[3] During many of these tasks, the ship rang with the voices of sailors of modest musical ability as they tried to lessen the boredom of repetitive jobs by chanting the songs of their home villages.

As he did his work, Gonzalo would have been reassured by another sound so familiar to voyagers of the period: prayers sung out by the pages. The severe dangers and uncertainties of sea travel in the age of sail had made sailors the most religious of any workers outside monastery or nunnery walls. Thus, a day at sea began with a recitation of *Pater Noster* and *Ave Maria* and an additional prayer of invocation for a safe voyage: "God give us good days, good voyage, good passage to the ship.... Let there be a good voyage; many good days may God grant your graces, gentlemen of the afterguard and gentlemen forward."[4] The remainder of the day was punctuated by religious observances repeated at almost every half-hour turning of the *ampolleta*. Shortly after sunset, the ship's entire company was called to prayers: the saying of the *Pater Noster*, *Ave Maria*, and *Credo* and the singing of the *Salve Regina*. "Singing" is perhaps a generous term for the muddle of dissonant sounds, what Salazar called "a confusion of bawlings," but few beseechers were ever more sincere than the sailors giving voice to the hope that God would grant them safe passage across the Ocean Sea.

It is easy to imagine Gonzalo, barefoot as was the sailors' practice and bearded after nearly two months at sea, sitting on the deck or standing at a rail and contemplating life. Seemingly endless weeks of the strange mixture of monotony and danger have pushed Palos, his family, and his friends far into the past, and the recent sighting of land birds on their fall migration through the Caribbean islands has sparked his eagerness to catch sight of the New World. The prevailing, easterly trade winds and Atlantic currents have taken the Spanish fleet to the edge of the Leeward Islands, a mountainous volcanic chain that separates the Atlantic Ocean from the Caribbean Sea.

Skirting the Leewards, the vessels enter the Caribbean through the Mona Passage, a 130-kilometre stretch of water between Hispaniola and what is now known as the island of Puerto Rico.

The dangers of the high seas have been overcome, but the passage is one of the most treacherous stretches of water in the Caribbean, itself a notoriously unpredictable body of water, and it has already claimed a number of Spanish ships. Operating with only rudimentary maps, navigators are further challenged by constantly shifting tidal currents generated by the islands on each side and by the sand shoals stretching far out from either shore. Once safely through the passage, the ships work their way along the south coast of Hispaniola until they arrive at Santo Domingo, an outpost located at a spot claimed by Columbus on his first voyage, in 1492.

The broad mouth of the Ozama River made Santo Domingo an excellent, sheltered port from which to command exploration of the Caribbean, and it became the first European settlement in the Spanish Indies. By the time that Gonzalo arrived, the population had grown to about 1,500, and there were port facilities, administration offices, military quarters, rough churches with thatched roofs, and rudimentary houses for settlers and others seeking their fortunes. Like frontier towns anywhere—in Alaska or California during the gold rushes, the western United States during the land rush, or the Australian Outback during its colonization—Santo Domingo had drawn a wide assortment of adventurers and soldiers of fortune. There were young sons of the gentry seeking the fortunes that they had been denied at home, civil officials, craftsmen, clerics, and soldiers mustered out of the army.

Crowding the narrow streets of Santo Domingo was also an assortment of rascals, rogues, and reprobates. Gonzalo might not have identified those who, having worked their way across the ocean, had jumped ship on their arrival, nor would he have known which were debtors putting themselves out of reach of their Castilian creditors. Unmistakable, though, were the figures with mutilated noses and ears: desperate men who had been punished for robbery back in Castile. Indeed, said Miguel de Cervantes, such men—and some women—had turned the Spanish Indies into "the shelter and refuge of Spain's *desperados*, the church of the lawless, the safe haven of murderers, the native land and cover for cardsharps, the general lure for loose women, the common deception of many and the particular remedy of few."[5]

Wandering through Santo Domingo, Gonzalo would have seen a great many more of the brown-skinned men and women paraded through the streets of Palos on Columbus's triumphant return in 1492. These were the indigenous people of Hispaniola and what is now Cuba and Jamaica, the Tainos, highly skilled farmers and fishers who had developed a sophisticated social structure and religion. They were, moreover, a remarkably open and generous people, which Columbus had commented on repeatedly in his journals:

> They are very gentle and without knowledge of what is evil; nor do they murder or steal.... There can be no better or gentler people.... All the people show the most singular loving behavior and they speak pleasantly.... They love their neighbors as themselves, and they have the sweetest talk in the world, and are gentle and always laughing.[6]

Had Gonzalo arrived with Columbus seventeen years earlier, he would have seen them in much larger numbers and in much happier conditions. Estimates of the Taino population at first contact with Europeans vary widely from 8 million to 200,000, but most historians agree that by 1510 there were only 35,000 people on Hispaniola.[7] By the middle of the sixteenth century, the Tainos would disappear entirely.

The overwhelming cause of their disappearance was the introduction to their world of European diseases such as smallpox, influenza, measles, and typhus, for which they had no immunity. To this onslaught was added their enslavement by the Spanish, both for working in Hispaniola and for cheap labour in Europe. Many a settler whose status and fortune were miserable back in Castile fancied himself a gentleman with a bit of land and some

Taino slaves to do the hard labour, or he could play the part of the business master and use them as pearl divers or forced labour in mines. However they were used as slaves, the Tainos were severely abused by their Spanish owners, suffering frequent beating, torture, and amputation of limbs as punishment for perceived lack of cooperation or production. Resistance, wrote Las Casas, was met with brutal retaliation: "The Spaniards made a rule among themselves that for every Christian slain by the Indians, they would slay a hundred Indians."[8]

Not all interaction between the Spanish and the Tainos was as cruel, but the relationship was nonetheless exploitative and underpinned by violence. If Gonzalo ventured out of Santo Domingo into the countryside, then he would have got his first glimpse of what, for a young man fresh from Palos, was an unusual sight: Taino women having sex with Spanish men and bearing them children, the first of that huge Central and South American ethnic group later to be known as *mestizos*: the offspring of European and indigenous parents.

With a shortage of Spanish women on Hispaniola, it was inevitable that the men of Castile would turn to Taino women and girls for sexual satisfaction. Although cohabitation with natives was considered an abomination by many Spanish officials and clerics, a number of settlers and prospectors took mistresses in a process of seduction that was hardly delicate. Miguel de Cuneo, who accompanied Columbus on his second voyage to the Indies, left a graphic description of his rape of a beautiful young native woman whom he had been given, as was the custom, by the great navigator. When, alone and naked in his cabin, she resisted his advances, he "took a rope end and thrashed her well, following which she produced such screaming and wailing as would cause you not to believe your ears. Finally we reached an agreement such that, I can tell you, she seemed to have been raised in a veritable school of harlots."[9] Such was the first recorded depiction of sexual interaction between the conquerors and the conquered.

If rape grew into cohabitation, then native women were forced to convert to Catholicism and given Spanish names, a practice that became common wherever the conquistadors went in the New World. Desperate men could thus persuade themselves that they were not truly living with a savage or heathen. In the rarer cases of actual marriage, conversion was mandatory, though such gestures of legality rarely earned the women any security or rights.

Violence and suffering on Hispaniola, however, were not limited to the natives. If Gonzalo had stepped off a ship nine years earlier, he would have noticed the decomposing bodies of two men hanging from gallows on each bank of the Ozama River. A week earlier he would have spotted seven such corpses, and a week later he would have seen two more. These were not the remains of troublesome Tainos but those of his own people, disaffected Spaniards who had rebelled against the brutal and autocratic governorship of Columbus and his brother Bartholomew. It was a rebellion that eventually led to the Admiral of the Ocean Sea, Bartholomew, and a third brother, Diego, being sent back to Spain in chains and stripped of their offices.

The rebellion on Hispaniola and the arrest of the Columbus brothers were dramatic examples of the fundamental and seemingly innate failing of the Spanish colonial enterprise in the New World. Because exploration was carried out not by a government office but by individual entrepreneurs with licences to explore and exploit as long as they gave the crown its share (the king's fifth), intense competition and jealousy were inevitable. From the settling of Hispaniola to Cortés's creation of an empire in Mexico to Pizarro's defeat of the Inca in Peru, the forces of the Spanish invasion were always marked by backbiting, infighting, betrayal, and murder. Not even the most distinguished of conquistadors—Columbus, Cortés, Balboa, or Pizarro—was immune from the treachery of envious or greedy rivals. An ordinary seaman like Gonzalo would have to keep his head down and his wits about him in this rapacious environment, especially the remote one to which he was headed.

On his voyage of discovery in 1492, Columbus had written of the Indies in glowing terms, and as late as 1498 he had claimed that Hispaniola "abounds in everything, especially in bread and meat. There is no lack of anything except wine and clothing. Of our people here, each has two or three Indians to serve him and dogs to hunt for him and, though it perhaps should not be said, women so handsome to be a wonder."[10] On his first voyage, he might have sincerely thought that he had discovered paradise in the New World, but as time went by his reports became more like propaganda than anything resembling the truth. He had promised Ferdinand and Isabella a profitable route to the Far East, and, failing to find Cathay or India, he made sure that he painted the opportunities for riches in Hispaniola in the most vivid colours. This idea of a new Eden across the Ocean Sea filtered down to the Castilian population as a whole and fired the imaginations of thousands of young men like Gonzalo.

By the time that he would have arrived in Santo Domingo, however, Hispaniola was anything but a paradise. The gold that natives had given to Columbus in 1492 proved to be little more than the modest gleanings from a land without many real veins of the precious mineral, and the mines managed by the Spanish settlers produced only meagre results. Only when Cortés had conquered the Aztecs and Pizarro the Incas did the conquistadors find enough of the gold with which they were obsessed.

In the meantime, the Spaniards, most of whom had invested all of their capital—and in some cases the dowries of their wives—with the intention of getting rich quickly or becoming eminent landowners on Hispaniola, soon became disillusioned. The oppressive heat and humidity bred not only fatigue but also disease-bearing mosquitoes, and hundreds of settlers died in a succession of epidemics. Dysentery and syphilis killed many others, and crop failures and an unwillingness to adopt a diet of indigenous fruits and vegetables led to famine and starvation. As well, the shrinking of the Taino population and the growing hostility among the remainder meant that the Spanish had to find cheap labour by importing slaves from adjoining islands and even from Africa. This was not the dream that had drawn men from Palos, Seville, or Sanlúcar—Cortés later remarked that "I came here to get rich, not to till the soil like a peasant"[11]—and many a defeated man made the long, miserable voyage back home.

The more resolute and adventurous among them, however, went to nearby islands—today Puerto Rico, Cuba, Jamaica, and the Bahamas—in search of gold and a more benign environment. Thus, by the time that Gonzalo's ship reached Hispaniola, that settlement had been abandoned by the most serious fortune seekers, and the importance of Santo Domingo had shrunk to that of an administrative centre and a refitting and restocking stopover for expeditions to other places. The most ambitious and risky of all these ventures was the one on which Gonzalo was embarked: the creation of the first European colony on the American mainland.

Eight years earlier an expedition led by a young merchant explorer, Rodrigo de Bastidas, had sailed along the north coast of South America, skirting what is now Venezuela and Colombia, and got as far as the Isthmus of Panama. Returning to Hispaniola, however, proved to be much more difficult since damage from *teredos*, the rapacious "shipworms" common in the Caribbean, caused his vessels to wreck off the west coast of Hispaniola and forced him to walk 200 miles through the jungle to Santo Domingo. Bastidas, however, brought back enough emeralds, pearls, and gold to excite Spanish investors. Two years later Columbus himself set out to explore the Central American shoreline, but he found the Caribbean little kinder to him than it had been to Bastidas. Attempting to cross treacherous water from Jamaica, he recalled, he was battered by savage weather:

Rain, thunder, and lightning were so continuous that it seemed the end of the world.... This intolerable storm continued in such a way that we saw neither the sun nor the stars as a guide. The ships were lying open to the skies, the sails broken, the anchors and shrouds lost, as were the cables....Many supplies went overboard; the crews were all sick and all were repenting their sins and turning to God. Everyone made vows, and promised to make pilgrimages if they were saved from death, and, very often, men went so far as to confess to each other. We had experienced other storms but none had been so terrifying. Many who we had thought were brave men were reduced to terror on more than one occasion.[12]

The little fleet survived the tempests, and, armed with charts from the Bastidas voyage and his undying conviction that he could still find the elusive passage to the Orient, Columbus made his own reconnaissance of the Isthmus of Panama. He, too, lost several ships to the *teredos*, but eventually he got back to Santo Domingo with stories of gold fields as far as the eye could see and of a land with excellent harbours, a fertile landscape, and gentle native inhabitants. It was, in fact, one of the least promising places in Central America in which to build a settlement.

The Spanish were not to discover this unfortunate truth until Gonzalo's expedition sailed there in 1509. Ferdinand had granted Diego de Nicuesa the territory, to be called Veragua, from the Gulf of Darién, at the south end of the Isthmus, northward. He had also given Alonso de Hojeda, an experienced conquistador who had sailed with Columbus and Amerigo Vespucci, the land to be named Urabá, south of the gulf extending into South America. Gonzalo was a member of the Hojeda venture, either in the original sailing or in a later vessel that came to its rescue when it became beleaguered, but either way he endured enormous hardship and privation that tested his mettle and might well have sapped his enthusiasm for overseas adventure.

Hojeda's party, 300-men strong, was the first to leave Santo Domingo, on November 12, 1509, and the first to run into trouble.

Landing at the site of the future city of Cartagena, Colombia, Hojeda boldly went ashore to claim the territory and make preparations for a colony. He did this against the advice of his pilot, Juan de la Cosa, who had twice sailed with Columbus, Vespucci, and Bastidas, and who knew that the local people, having heard graphic tales of Spanish brutality, were particularly resistant to conquest. Nearly 1,000 of their soldiers met the Spanish invasion with arrows dipped in *wurari*, a poison so toxic that anyone it touched met an agonizing death. His men routed, Hojeda, "flying as if on wings" according to one chronicler,[13] managed to escape into the jungle and was later found by other survivors with, it was said, the marks of 300 arrows on his shield. La Cosa, who had bravely stayed to cover his master's retreat, was less lucky, and the next morning his body, grotesquely bloated to twice its size and "as full of arrows as a hedgehog," was found tied to a tree.[14] Even battle-hardened adventurers among the Spanish could not bear to look at it.

Fortunately for the Hojeda party, Nicuesa's ships had arrived in Colombia at the same time on their way westward to his own land, and, though they were rivals, the two men joined forces to take revenge on the native attackers, looting the nearest village and killing every man, woman, and child they found. This done, Nicuesa moved on to the Isthmus of Panama, and Hojeda continued along the coast until he reached the east side of the Gulf of Darién, where he planted the banner of Castile and Leon and, with several hundred followers, declared the site to be the settlement of San Sebastián de Urabá.

From its inception, San Sebastián was beset by severe difficulties. Food supplies were soon exhausted or rotten in the tropical conditions, and resistance among local people made foraging in the jungle nearly impossible. Hojeda himself was hit in the thigh with a number of poisoned arrows and was saved only by having his gaping wounds seared shut by the pressure of white-hot irons. Men died of starvation, disease borne by the ever-present clouds of mosquitoes killed others, and the survivors were left weakened by fever. Crocodiles, a new and horrifying creature to the Spanish, ate one of the colony's mares, reducing the number of precious horses and lessening the animals' aura of terrifying invulnerability among the natives.

Desperate for help, Hojeda sent a ship back to Hispaniola to urge a friend, Bernardino de Talavera, to bring supplies and volunteers. In May 1510, Talavera arrived in a *nao* with cassava, bacon, and other foods, and when he left he took Hojeda, who intended to make a quick provisioning trip and return to San Sebastián. Once at sea, however, Hojeda discovered that his friend was in fact a pirate, the first of many brigands who would make travel on the Caribbean even more hazardous. Talavera had brazenly stolen the *nao* that he was commanding, and he proceeded to imprison Hojeda and seize his gold. Before he could enjoy his plunder, though, a hurricane destroyed the ship off the coast of Cuba, and the few remaining survivors, without any of the treasure, barely made it to shore. Found by a passing vessel, Talavera was taken to Jamaica, where he was quickly tried and hanged, and Hojeda made it back to Santo Domingo, where he remained until he died five years later.

When Hojeda had left for Hispaniola, he gave over command of San Sebastián to his second-in-command, a hardened, experienced soldier of fortune named Francisco Pizarro. Even more than most of the Spaniards who sailed to the New World, Pizarro had good reasons to think that his only chance at a decent life lay in exploration. Born in poverty in the province of Extremadura in 1471, he was one of four illegitimate sons of a professional soldier who did almost nothing for his children. Pizarro was not sent to school and never learned to read or write, and he grew up working as a swineherd. Desperate to escape a life that promised nothing, he joined the army, became an excellent soldier, and distinguished himself in action in Italy. Almost inevitably, the tales of riches to be found in the Spanish Indies seduced him, and in 1502 he sailed there under Alonso de Hojeda, with whom he remained for the exploration of the newly discovered lands around the Gulf of Darién.

To Gonzalo and the other members of the ill-fated settlement at San Sebastián, Pizarro was a commanding presence: tall, slender, and powerfully built. In some paintings, his hollow cheeks and thin beard suggest Don Quixote, but he was far from being the madly idealistic would-be knight of Cervantes. Although cool and calculating, and not given to making animated speeches, he was resourceful, efficient, fearless in battle, and resolute when he had made a decision. He was also cunning, unsympathetic to weakness in his men and defiance in his enemies, and tough to the point of brutality, traits that would one day make him one of the most savage and successful of the great conquistadors.

In Hojeda's absence, Pizarro held his band together as well as he could for several months, but deaths from disease, starvation, and wounds reduced its numbers to about eighty desperate men and a few women. With no rescue in sight, he decided to abandon San Sebastián in the summer of 1510, and the party began to work its way eastward in two ships along the coast back to Hispaniola. One craft carrying forty people was blown badly off course and wrecked along the coast of Cuba; only three survivors were ever found, and they were in captivity to a native tribe. Pizarro and forty-one others—one of whom was likely Gonzalo—in the other vessel had the good fortune to meet the long-awaited rescue mission. Hojeda, though he had little desire to return to the hardships of his colony, had commissioned two vessels commanded by Martín Fernández de Enciso to take the badly needed provisions and 152 new settlers to Urabá.

Any joy that Pizarro's men felt at the arrival of aid was quickly shattered when Enciso accused them of desertion and ordered them to return to San Sebastián with him and the new settlers. Not one individual had any desire to relive the hardships and horrors of life there, but Enciso had been given authority by Hojeda, and in late September the little flotilla entered the Gulf of Darién, where-upon the flagship immediately ran onto shoals and was wrecked. To add to the misery, the fort and the thirty shacks that had been abandoned had been burned by the natives, and the settlement had to be entirely rebuilt. Before long, the familiar pattern of isolation, antagonistic natives, disease, famine, and despair once again struck San Sebastián, and Enciso was not the man to lead in such desperate conditions.

Fortunately, the colony had two capable leaders: Pizarro and, rather surprisingly, a stowaway on Enciso's ship, Vasco Núñez de Balboa. Like Pizarro, Balboa was in his thirties and from Extremadura, and he had sailed with Bastidas on his voyage of discovery of the Isthmus of Panama. When Bastidas was unable to mount another expedition, Balboa remained on Hispaniola, where he was granted some land along the southwest coast. For nearly a decade, he raised hogs, which should have been a profitable venture, but he managed to get himself deeply into debt. By 1510, hounded by creditors and needing to get away, he arranged with a friend to be smuggled aboard one of Enciso's ships in a barrel normally used for flour. He took only the clothes on his back, his sword, and his battle-scarred yellow mastiff, Leoncico, a dog that proved to be so talented and fearsome in combat that he was made a corporal and earned several thousand pieces of gold in salary for his master.

Once at sea and safely out of sight of Santo Domingo, Balboa came out of hiding to face an enraged Enciso, who believed that the stowaway deserved the death penalty. Before the commander could carry out this sentence, however, he was persuaded that an experienced and capable fighter, especially one who possessed some knowledge of the coast, would be a valuable addition. Balboa, in the words of one Spanish historian, was

> tall, robust, of a noble disposition, and a prepossessing coun-tenance; his age did not then exceed five-and-thirty years,

and his singular vigour of frame rendered him capable of any degree of fatigue; his was the firmest arm, his was the strongest lance, his was the surest arrow....Nor did the endowments of his mind disgrace those of his body; ever active, vigilant, of unequalled penetration, and possessing the most invincible perseverance and constancy.[15]

Such qualities became obvious to everyone as conditions in San Sebastián became ruinous and somewhat anarchic under the inept leadership of Enciso. Balboa, with Pizarro as his right-hand man, took charge. The only man among them who had travelled the coast with Bastidas, Balboa was able to persuade the colony that the land to the west, across the Gulf of Darién, had a better harbour, better soil, and fewer troublesome natives. Thus, in November 1510, San Sebastián was abandoned, and, after driving out a local tribe, the Spanish established a new settlement called Santa Mariá de la Antigua del Darién, the first colonial capital on what came to be called Tierra Firme: that is, mainland America. Darién soon became the name given to the whole region at the southern part of the Isthmus of Panama.

Relocating the colony on territory that had been originally granted to rival Diego de Nicuesa was provocative, and it was only a few months before Nicuesa asserted his rights. His colony up the coast of the Isthmus of Panama, created a bit later than Hojeda's, had fared even worse in the face of the formidable mixture of hostile natives, rampant disease, and famine. In one year, he lost 380 settlers, and when the starving men—by then only a few score— began to eat their dead compatriots, Nicuesa pleaded for help from Santo Domingo. Help did not arrive; however, when one of his ships encountered two vessels from the new Darién settlement working their way along the coast, he believed that salvation had come.

Nicuesa, however, was a remarkably foolish man, entirely unsuited to the unscrupulous and vicious infighting that took place everywhere in the Spanish Indies, and he was especially unsuited to deal with the crafty Balboa. On being told of the settlement at Santa María, Nicuesa boldly announced plans to assume command of it, reform its governing structure, and take possession of any gold that it had collected. He would move his colony and arrive in Darién, like a victorious Roman general, in triumph before a grateful throng.

Balboa had other ideas. Having been told of Nicuesa's grandiose plan, he discussed the matter with the Darién officials, all of whom then vowed in a quasi-legal ceremony to reject any intrusion. Told of this resistance on his arrival at the harbour at Santa María, Nicuesa first claimed his rights and then, seeing that the power and authority lay with Balboa, was reduced to pleading to be accepted as merely a companion. When the suspicious colonists rejected even this request, Nicuesa accused them of encroaching on his territory, of committing treason against the crown, and even of defying God himself. Realizing finally, on March 1, 1511, that all doors were firmly shut against him, he sailed out of the Gulf of Darién with seventeen of his men. Swallowed up by the treacherous Caribbean waters, nothing was ever again seen or heard of Nicuesa, his ship, or his crew.

A month or so later Balboa dealt with Enciso with the same cunning that he had used to dispatch Nicuesa. The foolish demand by Enciso that he be given the largest share of the gold amassed to that point was met by an investigation of his usurpation of authority and attempted misappropriation of the treasure. Expelled from Santa María, he left in bitterness for Hispaniola and thence for Spain, where he complained to the Court of Ferdinand about Balboa's seizing of power. Left with complete control of Darién, Balboa became known as "the first *caudillo* ['commander'] of the New World."[16]

When Nicuesa departed from the colony, some members of his original party remained behind, preferring the hardships and privations of Darién to the risks of putting out to sea with their hapless leader. Among them was a man whose name would become inextricably linked with that of Gonzalo Guerrero and who would play an important role in one of Spain's greatest colonial conquests. A twenty-year-old from the Andalusian town of Écija, Jerónimo de Aguilar had received some religious training—probably in a Franciscan seminary—and might have gone to the New World on the pretext of responding to Queen Isabella's wish that the savages of the New World be saved from their heathenism. Since there is little evidence of his saving any souls while there, it is just as likely that he had grown restive in the highly ordered religious life of Castile or was escaping from some blot on his record. In any case, he joined the Nicuesa expedition to Veragua, and, like Gonzalo in Urabá, Aguilar was one of the few survivors of that ill-fated colony.

Whatever their different reasons for going to the New World, and no matter whether they had endured life in Veragua or Urabá, Jerónimo and Gonzalo had one thing in common: they could not have enlisted in more ill-advised colonizing ventures. In almost every way, the attempt to create settlements or to find great amounts of gold and other treasure around the Gulf of Darién was disastrous. As a site for a colony, the Spanish businessmen-adventurers could hardly have found a less promising region in central America:

> Darién had no decent harbor, no large rivers, little arable land. It dominated no trade routes, actual or potential. Ships had a hard time reaching it and a worse one getting away, and for any vessel too big to beach easily a stopover was fatal. Its climate was unhealthy and (most damning of all in that age) its mineral resources were insignificant. As if to complete the picture, its settlement, Santa María del Antigua, was tucked away in a narrow, rather marshy valley five miles from the sea—a strategically inapt location where it was impossible to produce food for more than a few hundred people.[17]

So unsuitable did Darién prove to be as a settlement site that finally in 1519 Santa María was abandoned, and a new capital was established miles away at a more propitious location. Even the name of Darién was transferred to territory north and west, where today it refers to a province of Panama. The jungle reclaimed the first site of Santa María, and 500 years later the original Darién remains sparsely populated and without any thriving community.

The promise of gold had brought the Spanish to Darién: stories of nuggets as big as oranges, streams so richly laden with flakes that one fished for them with nets, and fields where one needed only to burn off the grass to uncover enough gold to plate one's roof. These expectations were fed by natives who, recognizing the insatiable hunger of the Spanish for gold, told them of such riches—always, of course, farther off in another territory—and by conquistadors such as Bastidas and Columbus who exaggerated the prospects to please their king and their investors. Such hopes proved to be as overstated as the environment was inhospitable. In the decade from 1511 to 1520, the Spanish took out only an estimated 41,000 pesos of gold, a disappointing return on hundreds of prospecting ventures and numerous thefts of native jewellery and relics. If Gonzalo and his fellows in Santa María had golden dreams, then they would have to venture beyond Darién into the Isthmus of Panama to realize them. And, though this hunger for gold would remain largely unsatisfied, it would lead them to one of the most astonishing discoveries in the New World.

In the spring of 1511, Balboa led a party of exploration northwest into an adjoining territory called Careta and beyond it into Comogre. In both places, he was provided with food and, as signs of friendship, artwork fashioned in gold. When the Spaniards immediately began melting down the pieces and weighing the gold, an appalled son of the chief of Comogre condemned them for their greed, telling them that he could show them a land where the people drank out of golden goblets and where gold was as cheap as iron. From this place, added the native, they could look out over another sea, one on which sailed ships as large as those of the Spanish.

That the Spanish explorers were received relatively amiably in Careta and Comogre was a tribute to Balboa and could not have escaped the notice of Gonzalo. Under Hojeda, he saw, and probably participated in, the subjugation and slaughter of large numbers of natives, and, with the arrival of Enciso and Balboa, he witnessed the kind of vicious infighting that had earlier plagued Hispaniola. He saw the cunning Balboa rise from stowaway fleeing from bad debts to become one of the joint *alcaldes*, or "mayors," of Santa María and within months to be the sole ruler of the settlement. He saw, too, the clever manipulation and expulsion of Nicuesa and Enciso, which left Balboa in command of both the colonies that were to have been Urabá and Veragua.

Balboa was a masterful plotter, and he could be ruthless in his treatment of uncooperative natives. As he settled into his role of *caudillo* of Darién, however, he showed a talent for dealing with the natives in a manner rarely seen in the Spanish Indies. Instead of relying entirely on displays of brute force, on the butchering and enslaving of the tribes, he negotiated with the chiefs and persuaded them that they should share their land, that he could defeat their enemies and ensure peace, and that he would keep abuse of their people by the Spanish soldiers to a minimum. Such diplomacy was noted with admiration by at least one colonial official reporting to the Spanish court:

Vasco Nuñez had labored with very good skill to make peace with many caciques ["chiefs"] and principal lords of the Indians, by which he kept in peace about thirty caciques with all their Indians, and did so by not taking more from them than they were willing to give, helping them to resolve quarrels one with another, and thereby Vasco Nuñez became so well liked that he could go in security through a hundred leagues of Tierra Firme. In all parts the Indians willingly gave him much gold and also their sisters and daughters to take with him to be married or used as he wished. By these means peace was spread and the revenue of Your Highness greatly increased.[18]

In one matter, the treatment of the women given to him by the chiefs, Balboa might have had a profound influence on Gonzalo and his future relationships with the natives. Having captured the *cacique* of Careta, Balboa came to a political arrangement that satisfied his prisoner—particularly since it involved the Spanish protecting his tribe from its enemies—and, as a pledge of friendship, Balboa was given the *cacique*'s daughter as his wife. Little is known of her, and over the centuries she has been made a romantic figure, a beautiful young maiden, a "princess" with the name Caretita or Cacica who became the conquistador's bride.

Witnesses reported that the woman was indeed beautiful and, being the daughter of the *cacique*, had some status in her community, but she was almost certainly very young, perhaps only fourteen. Like her father, she was a captive, and Balboa, as was the custom with the conquistadors throughout the Spanish Indies, could simply have taken her as his mistress and discarded her when he wished. Even more common was the practice among the Spanish settlers of simply going into the jungle and raping native women. Balboa, however, found the young girl so attractive that he underwent a tribal marriage ritual, likely a simple joining of hands and an invocation of whatever deity to bless the union; but it was not a Catholic ceremony. And for the rest of Gonzalo's days in the colony, and for several years thereafter, Balboa, notwithstanding his taking of other native mistresses and his eventual betrothal to the daughter of a fellow Spaniard, treated Caretita with affection, care, and respect.

In the autumn of 1511, Gonzalo must have thought Palos and Andalusia very far away, both geographically and temporally. He was a very different man from the one who had sailed out of the harbour at Cadiz with dreams, whether chivalric or material, of creating a successful life in the New World. Balboa, a capable and in many ways admirable leader seemingly on the verge of discovering the long-sought El Dorado, must have looked to Gonzalo like someone to follow. Such a path would have brought a young man more glory than riches, but it would also have been fraught with danger.

In September 1511, Balboa, in search of the "Kingdom of Gold" that he had been told lay to the south and west, led a party of his men on a strenuous trek across the narrowest part of the Isthmus of Panama. After a fortnight's journey, he was able to stand on the crest of a hill and become the first European in history to view the Pacific Ocean from the east. As his men joined him on the peak in a prayer of thanks, in the words of the famous sonnet by John Keats, they "look'd at each other with a wild surmise" at the staggering implications of their discovery.[19] As had gradually come to be suspected, Tierra Firme was not the Orient but a whole new continent unknown to anyone except its own inhabitants.

Balboa thus joined the ranks of the greatest European discoverers: Columbus, Cortés, Magellan, de Gama, Pizarro, and Ponce de Leon. But, like so many of Spain's most illustrious conquistadors—Columbus, Cortés, and Pizarro—his achievement was not enough to guarantee a life of affluence and acclaim from his countrymen. Indeed, it was not enough to ensure that he had a life at all. Because of the persistent complaints of Enciso, Ferdinand appointed a new governor of the colony, and little more than five years after his momentous discovery Balboa was arrested on charges of trying to overthrow the new administration, and in January 1519 he and four of his followers were beheaded.

Had Gonzalo followed Balboa to his sighting of the South Sea and his subsequent explorations, he might have had to step carefully to avoid the fate of the four men who went with the conquistador to the block. To do so, he would have needed only to emulate Pizarro, who, after loyally serving Balboa for eight years, commanded the force that arrested and delivered him to the governor, thereby avoiding any implication that he himself had been part of any insurgency.

Having survived the arrest of Balboa and his men, Gonzalo might have followed Pizarro to another of the greatest discoveries and conquests in the New World. In 1530, Pizarro was granted royal permission for an expedition to Peru and authority over any lands that he might capture, a venture that finally found the staggering riches for which Spaniards had hungered since 1492. It led, as well, to the brutal overthrow of the Inca Empire, the treacherous execution of its emperor, Atahualpa, and the near obliteration of the Inca culture. Like Balboa, however, Pizarro had only a few years to enjoy his triumph before he became another Spaniard killed by his own people: in 1541, he was assassinated by the aggrieved son of a rival leader whom he had executed after defeating him in battle.

Gonzalo, however, was not given the opportunity to follow either of the famed conquistadors. In November 1511, following three months of storms and heavy rains, the colony at Santa María suffered a crop failure, a calamity made much worse by the depletion of any food brought in earlier from Santo Domingo. Confronted with imminent famine, Balboa decided to send one of his right-hand men, the *regidor* Juan de Valdivia, to seek not only provisions from Hispaniola but also 500 to 1,000 experienced men together with the necessary arms and ammunition. To impress the government officials in Santo Domingo, Valdivia took with him the king's *quinto*, the "fifth" of all treasure due to the royal court, in this case 150 pounds of gold. Loaded as well with the treasure of private adventurers, his ship was the richest yet to sail the Caribbean.

When Valdivia left Darién on January 13, 1512, he travelled with a number of passengers. One of them was the cleric Jerónimo de Aguilar, who had survived the travails of the Nicuesa enterprise and who was happy to seize the opportunity to return to the relative comforts of Hispaniola and perhaps even Spain. Among the seamen manning the ship was Gonzalo, but history does not record whether he, too, was working his way back to Santo Domingo and thence home to Palos or whether he intended to return with the freshly supplied vessel to Darién.

Whatever their intentions, neither man made it back to Hispaniola. When their ship sailed out of the Gulf of Darién, it was the last that anyone ever saw of it, Juan de Valdivia, and most of his passengers and crew members. Once again the formidable hazards of the Caribbean swallowed up a Spanish vessel. And it would be more than seven years before Spanish officials learned what had happened on the ill-fated voyage.

CHAPTER FOUR

"It Will Never Do to Leave Him Here":
SHIPWRECK, ENSLAVEMENT, AND HERNÁN CORTÉS

Noble sirs: I left Cuba with a fleet of eleven ships and 500 Spaniards, and laid up at Cozumel, whence I write this letter. Those of the island have assured me that there are in the country five or six men with beards and resembling us in all things. They are unable to give or tell me other indications, but from these I conjecture and hold certain that you are Spaniards. I and these gentlemen who go with me to settle and discover these lands urge that within six days from receiving this you come to us, without making further delay or excuse. If you shall come we will make due acknowledgement and reward the good offices which this armada shall receive from you. I send a brigantine that you may come in it, and two boats for safety.
—Hernán Cortés, 1519[1]

The extraordinary conquest of Mexico by Hernán Cortés began nineteen kilometres off the Yucatán Peninsula on Cozumel, the forty-five-kilometre-long island in the Caribbean Sea. It was there that the great conquistador unexpectedly found one of the most important weapons in his struggle to defeat the vast numbers of Aztec warriors who stood between him and possession of Montezuma's capital city of Tenochtitlán. That weapon was Jerónimo de Aguilar, who had miraculously survived a shipwreck and was living among the Maya. It was on Cozumel, too, that Cortés learned to his lasting regret that another Spanish castaway, Gonzalo Guerrero, had refused to follow Aguilar and join the Spanish forces.

Cortés chose to land at Cozumel because he knew that its inhabitants were much more hospitable than those on the peninsula itself. The distance from the mainland, made more pronounced by a dangerous current running along the coast, meant that the islanders lived somewhat isolated from the political intrigue and tribal warfare of other Maya. They had never fought against the Spanish intrusion, preferring to disappear into the dense tropical jungle. Cortés, through a combination of intimidation and skilful diplomacy, was able to persuade the local *cacique* ("chief"), Naum Pat, to cooperate with him, and Cozumel became the customary first stop for Spanish incursions into Mexico, a convenient and safe place to repair ships and take on fresh water, for the next 450 years.

Cortés knew of the fierce resistance of the mainland Maya and the relatively cooperative nature of the Cozumel natives from two earlier voyages made by the Spanish to the Yucatán Peninsula. In February 1517, the governor of Cuba, Diego Velázquez de Cuéllar, sent Francisco Hernández de Córdoba, with three ships and about 100 men, across the Caribbean on a slave-hunting and exploratory expedition. After about three weeks under sail, they reached the most northeastern point of the Yucatán Peninsula, which they named Cabo ("Cape") Catoche after being greeted by natives saying "*Cones cotoch,*" meaning "Come to our house." After giving the Maya gifts of green glass beads, and silk and woollen clothes, a good many of the party accepted the invitation and went ashore. Following an apparent welcome, the Maya suddenly ambushed the Hernández party, attacking them with missiles, darts, arrows, stones hurled by slings, and razor-sharp, obsidian-edged spears. Fifteen Spanish men were wounded, two of whom later died, and a dozen or so natives were killed by the Spaniards' swords, crossbows, and harquebuses (muzzle-loading firearms). The Spanish retreated to their ships with a respect for Mayan fighting skills and cunning.

The Spanish also took away from Cabo Catoche what they assumed was the name of the new land that they thought was an island. According to several chronicles, Hernández de Córdoba asked the natives what their country was called, and they responded by saying "*Uic athan*," which meant roughly "What do you say?" or "We do not understand you." When a Spanish scribe was ordered to write down the response, it became "Yucatán." Thus began centuries of Spanish misunderstanding of the indigenous peoples of Mexico.

Made wary by the ambiguous and ultimately hostile behaviour of the natives at Cabo Catoche, Hernández de Córdoba's company moved westward along the Gulf of Mexico coastline to Campeche, where they heard more strange sounds from the lips of the natives. They were words that would intrigue both the Spanish command back in Cuba and two subsequent expeditions to the Yucatán. The natives greeted Hernández de Córdoba's men by pointing in the direction of the sunrise and saying "*Castilan. Castilan.*"

Baffled by the words and intimidated by threatening behaviour at Campeche, Hernández sailed farther along the coast to a settlement near the modern town of Champotón, where the Mayan belligerence and puzzling references were repeated. The great chronicler of the early Spanish conquest of Mexico, Bernal Díaz del Castillo, describes the approach of native warriors as the Spanish were filling water casks:

> Their faces were painted black and white…and ruddled and they came in silence straight toward us, as though they came in peace, and by signs they asked us whether we came from where the sun rose, and we replied that we did come from

the direction of the sunrise. We were at our wits end consid-
ering the matter, and wondering what the words were which
the Indians called out to us for they were the same as those
used by the people of Campeche, but we never made out
what it was that they said.[2]

In the fierce battle that ensued, Hernández de Córdoba lost twenty
men. He then retraced his path to Cuba, where he reported his
findings to Velázquez, including the inexplicable repetition of
Castilan. Velázquez realized the potential importance of this new
land called Yucatán to Spain and to his own colonial ambitions,
and he soon ordered a new expedition to be led by another conquistador, Juan de Grijalva.

Grijalva sailed with four ships and 240 men, soldiers and settlers whose fortunes had not flourished in Cuba and who were
lured by tales of abundant gold in the Yucatán. After landing on
Cozumel in May 1518, the flotilla crossed to the mainland, where
they sighted the substantial towns of Xel Ha and Tulum, and continued around the peninsula into the Gulf of Mexico. Near a large
river that they christened Río de Grijalva, they met peacefully
with local natives, with whom they exchanged gifts—the Spanish
offering the customary glass beads and their hosts in return giving them food, clothing, and a few pieces of gold. When Grijalva
asked eagerly about the gold, he was told that there was much
more of it in the direction of the sunset, and, reported Díaz del
Castillo, "they said 'Colua, Colua, Méjico, Méjico,' but we did not
know what this Colua or Méjico could be."[3] The Spanish returned
to Cuba fired with the thought of golden riches to be found in the
interior of the new land.

Velázquez did not take long to mount a third Yucatán expedition, appointing Cortés, a thirty-three-year-old adventurer from
Medellín, to command it. Having been in Cuba for twelve years,
Cortés owned land and was a magistrate of the colony's capital,
but he burned with a desire to make his fortune in the newly

discovered lands to the west. So in February 1519 he set sail with the largest force yet dispatched to the Yucatán. His instructions were to establish colonies on territories discovered by Grijalva, to convert their inhabitants to Christianity, to map the coastline of the Yucatán, and to take possession of any new regions that he might find. He was also charged with investigating strange tales that had been brought back by the previous expeditions, stories suggesting that the natives possessed a mischievous sense of humour. There were places, it was said, inhabited by people with large, broad ears and others with faces like those of dogs, and there was said to be a town inhabited solely by women, Amazons, who had no need of men. And Cortés was to look into the curious shouts of "*Castilan*" heard by Hernández de Córdoba's men in various parts of the Yucatán.

In his investigation of that word, Cortés was aided by Díaz del Castillo and a fellow voyager who had been part of Hernández de Córdoba's party. Once settled on Cozumel, Cortés quizzed them about what they had witnessed. He decided to ask the chiefs on the island about the strange native utterances. They told him that they did indeed know of three or four bearded men who resembled those travelling with him; they were the slaves of several *caciques* living about a two-day journey away in the interior of Yucatán. Cortés decided to try to rescue them. On the advice of the *caciques*, he offered a ransom of coloured glass beads and composed a letter telling the slaves to come to him for repatriation within six days of receiving it.

Putting a message into the captives' hands was challenging because the Cozumel Mayan runners were terrified that they would be killed and eaten by the fierce *caciques* on the mainland. Several young men were finally bribed to risk being couriers only after Cortés had shown them how to travel without the letters being seen. He realized that a scrap of paper could easily be hidden in their thick black hair, which they wore long and braided over their foreheads. So several runners were dispatched into the Yucatán jungle.

Cortés anchored one of his brigantines off Cabo Catoche to await responses to his letter; when no Spanish captives appeared after six days, the ship returned to Cozumel. Disappointed, Cortés abandoned the idea of rescuing Spaniards and ordered his ships to move on along the course taken by Hernández de Córdoba and Grijalva. At Isla Mujeres, however, his main supply ship, full of the important cassava bread, whose value as a staple foodstuff the Spanish had learned from the Taino and which they had brought from Cuba, sprang a leak, and the flotilla returned to Cozumel for repairs. This "disaster" turned out to be the first in a series of strokes of good fortune. In an obsequious letter to the Spanish monarchs, Cortés called it "a great miracle and divine mystery, whereby we have come to believe that nothing can be undertaken in Your Majesties' service which does not end in good."[4]

When the ships were again seaworthy, everyone except Cortés and a few others embarked. As this small band prepared to be rowed to its craft, however, a storm blew up, and the flotilla remained at Cozumel for another night. The next day being Sunday, the departure was further delayed when Cortés insisted that mass be said. When the Spanish were again on the shore, they sighted a large Mayan canoe approaching from the mainland. A captain, Andrés de Tápia, was ordered to take some men and hide near the beach and to bring back any natives who might land. Four figures did step ashore at a nearby cove, completely naked except for loincloths, their hair braided and over their foreheads, and well armed with bows and arrows.

When Tápia's men rushed the group with swords drawn, three of the natives were so terrified that they ran for their canoe. The fourth, however, stepped forward and, in a language unknown to the Spaniards, told his fellows not to be afraid or to flee. Then, turning to the approaching swordsmen, he stunned them by asking, in "words badly articulated and worse pronounced, 'Gentlemen, are you Christians?'" When they replied that they were Spaniards, he burst into tears and exclaimed, "Dios y Santa María de Sevilla"

("God and Saint Mary of Seville"). Then, reported Cortés' secretary and biographer, Francisco López de Gómara,

> he asked if it was Wednesday, for he was accustomed to
> devoting several hours to prayer on that day, and he begged
> them to join him, sank to his knees, and raised his hands
> and eyes to Heaven. Then, with tears in his eyes, he offered
> up a prayer to God, giving him infinite thanks for His mercy
> in liberating him from those infidels and hellish men, and
> for restoring him to the Christians and men of his nation.[5]

When his prayers were done, the man was helped to his feet, embraced by Tápia and his fellows, and taken with his three Mayan companions along the beach to be questioned by Cortés. Word about this extraordinary figure who had come ashore quickly spread through the encampment, and a crowd pressed around him as he walked along the sand. As they approached Cortés' quarters, sailors and soldiers jostled with each other to get near enough to hear what he would say.

As he neared Cortés, the man stopped and made a deep reverential bow and then, with the three Maya, set his bow and arrows on the ground and squatted in the fashion of the natives. Putting their right hands in their mouths, they covered them with saliva, placed them on the ground, and then rubbed them over their hearts as a mark of respect, a signal that they were prostrating and humbling themselves like the earth on which they trod. Although the leader of the quartet, said Díaz del Castillo, had identified himself to Tápia, Cortés saw only four natives:

> He was naturally brown and he had his hair shorn like an
> Indian slave, and carried a paddle on his shoulder, he was
> shod with one old sandal and the other was tied to his belt,
> he had on a ragged old cloak, and a worse loin cloth, with
> which he covered his nakedness, and he had tied up, in a

bundle in his cloak, a Book of Hours, old and worn. When Cortés saw him in this state, he too was deceived like the other soldiers, and asked Tápia, "Where is the Spaniard?" On hearing this, the Spaniard squatted down on his haunches as the Indians do and said, "I am he."[6]

Cortés ordered him to be given a shirt, doublet, drawers, cape, and sandals, but the man did not find this gesture much of a kindness: he had become so accustomed to wearing almost nothing that he could hardly bear the constricting Spanish garb. Moreover, he ate and drank little of the ample meal provided to him because, having lived on a native diet for so long, he feared that his stomach would not easily adjust to eating Spanish food again.

When the man was comfortable, Cortés began to interrogate him, and, for the first time in seven years, the mystery of the disappearance of the Valdivia voyage was revealed. Struggling to pronounce his words, the strange figure explained that he was Jerónimo de Aguilar, a native of Écija who had taken holy orders and sailed to the New World and settled in Darién. He had joined Valdivia's expedition to Santo Domingo to inform the governor of the unrest, to recruit men and procure food, and to take 20,000 ducats to be sent to the king. They had successfully crossed the Caribbean and nearly reached Jamaica when calamity struck and their caravel was wrecked either upon the shoals called Las Víboras, "The Vipers," or a reef with the equally menacing name of Los Alacranes, "The Scorpions." With the ship aground and no longer seaworthy, twenty people—including several women—boarded a small boat without sails, one pair of very poor oars, and no bread or water. Without food and water—some were driven to drinking their urine—and with little protection from the searing heat of the Caribbean sun, it was not long before seven castaways died. They hoped to reach Jamaica or Cuba, but without sufficient oars they drifted for thirteen or fourteen days and then were swept onto the Yucatán coast by a strong and fast westerly current.

As soon as their boat touched shore, said Aguilar, the sick and weakened travellers clambered out of the boat but were immediately met by a swarm of hostile natives. In the scuffle that ensued, one Spaniard had his head split open by an obsidian-edged axe, and he ran holding his skull together into the dense jungle. In the weeks that followed, his wound was treated by a local woman, and he survived with a deep scar on his head but a deranged mind. He lived for three more years, tolerated as a *gracioso* ("fool") by the natives, who believed that he had been cured by the gods because only they had the power to heal such a terrible wound.

The remaining castaways were easily captured, and, according to Aguilar, Valdivia and four more were soon sacrificed and eaten by the natives in a celebratory feast. The seven others, caged and well fed like prized cattle, suspected that they were being fattened for future sacrificial ceremonies, so they broke out of their pen and fled into the jungle. Exhausted, confused, and frightened, they had the good fortune—God's will, said Aguilar—to be found by the men of a tribe called Xamanzana, the enemies of those from whom they were fleeing. Their *cacique*, Ah-kin Cuz, was a much more humane captor, granting the Spaniards their lives in return for their service as his slaves, an offer that they accepted with alacrity. This servitude, however, was so rigorous, and living conditions were so harsh and unfamiliar to most of the Spanish, that one by one all except Aguilar and a castaway whom he knew as Gonzalo soon died.

Why Aguilar and Gonzalo survived the hardships of living among such alien people as the Maya while their companions perished is a fascinating question. Physical strength and endurance would have been essential for survival in very unfamiliar conditions: a diet of exotic foods; shelter in what would have seemed like primitive hovels; a relentless onslaught of mosquitoes, "blood-sucking ticks" called *garrapatas*, and ants with a sting like a hornet; and the constant danger posed by the peninsula's poisonous snakes, crocodiles, and jaguars.

Survival in such conditions, though, would have required much more than mere physical resilience: it would have taken remarkable mental toughness. Indeed, Aguilar is reported to have told Cortés and his captains that some of his companions in captivity died from "grief," from which can be inferred despair, depression, and a sense of hopelessness. Such feelings would hardly be surprising in people cast up on an unknown shore, captured and enslaved by fierce natives, and facing the likelihood that they would never be rescued or see their homes and families again. Underlying it all must have been an overwhelming sense of dislocation, of culture shock, of being surrounded by a sea of unfamiliarity, not the least of which was a language that it would take time and considerable effort to learn. Only someone with a strong sense of self, will to live, or faith—religious or secular—could have avoided sinking into despair.

According to chronicler Francisco Cervantes de Salazar, simple self-preservation drove Aguilar in the early days of his captivity in Xamanzana. For the first three years, he was forced into heavy labour hauling wood and water on his back and lugging fish inland from the sea on narrow stony paths. This he did "with a joyful face in order to assure life, which is so beloved." Moreover, Aguilar performed his duties promptly and submissively, even interrupting his eating to carry out a command, and thus "won the heart and good will of his lord and all of those of his household and land."[7]

Aguilar's Mayan captors were not beyond using intimidation to ensure his obedience. One feast day, he said, some warriors were shooting with bows and arrows at an unfortunate dog that they had hung high in a tree, and one of their leaders grabbed him by the arm and said, "What do you think of these archers, how accurate they are, for he who aims at the eye, hits the eye, and he who aims at the mouth, hits the mouth?" Did the Spaniard think, if he were placed there, that they would miss any part of him? A modern Mafia don could not have arranged a more effective coercion, and Aguilar responded with the expected servility. "Lord," he replied, "I am thy slave and you can do what you wish with me, but you are so good that you will not wish to lose a slave like me who will serve you so well in what you may command."[8]

Aguilar, if his report to Cortés is to be believed, seems to have impressed the *cacique* of Xamanzana in another way. Having taken holy orders back in Spain, he was determined to live chastely and never looked on any of the comely village women with any sign of desire. Noticing this unusual behaviour, the *cacique* decided to test him one night by sending him on a fishing party to the coast with a beautiful girl as his companion. The pair was provided with one hammock in which to sleep before the dawn's fishing, and, after hanging it between two trees, the girl called to Aguilar to join her, but he lit a fire on the beach and lay down on the sand. From time to time, she called seductively to him, and other men in the party suggested that he was not a man because he preferred the cold sand to her warm embrace. Although severely tempted, he was determined to maintain a promise to God that he would not touch a pagan woman as long as God in return freed him from his captivity, so he did not yield. This resolute chasteness so impressed the *cacique* that he thereafter entrusted his wife and his household to Aguilar's care.

This story might be fanciful, but there can be little doubt that it was primarily his religious faith that allowed Aguilar to survive his captivity. Throughout all of his travails—the shipwreck, the days at sea, the captivity—he had clung to one possession, his breviary, a book of prayers with illustrations, and with it he was able to observe the Catholic feast days. He also prided himself on keeping track of the days on the Christian calendar, though by the time he stepped ashore to meet Cortés he was slightly mistaken, thinking that it was Wednesday rather than Sunday. After more than seven years in the Yucatán jungle, perhaps he could be forgiven for an error of three days. Aguilar and the Spanish chroniclers who followed him attributed his survival and deliverance to Cortés to divine intervention and to his steadfast belief in God's power to save him. A more secular explanation would be that, for someone adrift in unfamiliar circumstances, the breviary was a little island of order, organization, and familiarity.

But what of Aguilar's fellow survivor, Gonzalo? Aguilar told his rescuers that Gonzalo was living a considerable distance away, having been sold to another chief, Nachan Ka'an, of Chactemal. He got permission from his *cacique* to travel there—"five leagues distant"—to convey the letter from Cortés. On arrival, he read the letter to Gonzalo and urged him to go back with him and to his own people. To Aguilar's disappointment, Gonzalo replied,

> Brother Aguilar, I am married and have three children, and the Indians look upon me as a *cacique* and captain in war- time. You go and God be with you, but I have my face tattooed and my ears pierced, what would the Spanish say should they see me in this guise? And look how handsome these boys of mine are, for God's sake give me those green beads you have brought, and I will give the beads to them and say that my brothers have sent them from my own country.

Gonzalo's Mayan wife was far less diplomatic in her response, angrily shouting at their visitor: "What is this slave coming here for talking to my husband—go off with you, and don't trouble us with any more words."[9] With these curses ringing in his ears, and with surprise that a woman would speak to him in this manner, Aguilar regretfully returned to his own tribe and to his fateful meeting with the Cortés expedition.

In the years immediately following Aguilar's telling of this tale, Spanish chroniclers attempted to paint a fuller picture of it. Gonzalo was indeed living among the Maya in Chactemal, a chief- dom situated near the modern city of Chetumal, in a town called Ichpaatún, located at what are now the ruins of Oxtankah. He had, as he said to Aguilar, not only survived the rigours of enslavement but also, over the years, so impressed Nachan Ka'an that he became a respected member of the community and a military leader. He had married the *cacique*'s daughter, variously called Zazil Há, Xzamil, Zamil, Nicte-Ha, and Ixpilotzama. In some accounts, she is called Princess Nicte-Ha, meaning "Princess Water Lily," the source of inspiration for the modern romanticized version of the story in which the Spanish castaway marries a Mayan princess.

Aguilar told Cortés and his company that he had travelled five leagues to see Gonzalo, but historians have pointed out that this is at least an underestimation. Chactemal was located at the southernmost region of the Yucatán Peninsula, much farther from Aguilar's tribe than five leagues, a league traditionally being considered the distance of an hour's walk or five kilometres. To reach Gonzalo would have meant a trek of several hundred kilometres. If, as is unlikely, he was able to travel by canoe along the coast, then it would have been a long trip, but trudging through the dense jungle or along the rugged coastline would have taken days. Years earlier the Maya had constructed raised roads, called *sacbe*s or "white roads" because they were built of stone covered with limestone stucco, through the jungle, but there were few of them, and they connected only major centres. Aguilar and his native escort would thus have had to make the lengthy journey on foot through the narrow and winding trails, a rugged and exhausting march in the heat and mosquito-infested jungle and swamp.

His first sight of his former companion would have filled Aguilar with a mixture of recognition and shock. He would not have been surprised to see the figure before him, after seven years in Yucatán, with skin deeply tanned by prolonged exposure to the tropical sun, nor would he have thought it unusual that Gonzalo was clothed in only a loincloth and deerskin or hemp sandals. And he would not have considered it strange to see his friend with his hair long, braided, and worn over his forehead. Aguilar could have looked at himself and seen some of the same features.

But he would have looked with horror on Gonzalo's face. Where there had once been the familiar features of a fellow Andalusian, there was now a countenance covered with the striking tattoos, designed to impress friends and intimidate enemies, worn by Mayan men. Such markings, Aguilar knew, were sported only by married tribesmen or warriors. He would have seen, as well, Gonzalo's pierced ears, nose, and lower lip, adorned by various pieces of jewellery made of jade and other colourful stone and metal. If he had reached for Gonzalo's hand, he would have seen that it too was tattooed, an emblem of honour permitted only to Mayan men who had demonstrated their valour.

Aguilar would have looked as well at Gonzalo's Mayan wife and his half-caste children and been aghast. In the absence of women of their own race in the New World—in Darién, for example, where Aguilar had spent some months—the Spanish had taken native mistresses but only after the women had been baptized and given Spanish names. Gonzalo, however, had married a "savage" according to the rites of her "uncivilized" people.

Gonzalo had called his young sons "handsome," but that is not how they likely would have looked to his former compatriot. Coming to maturity in a land driven by rulers desiring racial purity, an emerging nation that had expelled Muslims and Jews in a fever of ethnic cleansing, Aguilar probably would have seen Gonzalo's offspring as savage bastards, illegitimate and abominable. Having sailed to the New World to convert the heathen to Catholicism and to settle it with enough countrymen to create a true "New Spain," one in which Spanish lords would rule over native slaves, he likely would have been appalled at witnessing the beginning of a corrupting miscegenation.

It is tempting to see Aguilar's confrontation with Gonzalo in terms of Marlow's discovery of the corrupted Kurtz, the idealistic Englishman who has "gone native," in the climactic scenes of Joseph Conrad's novella *Heart of Darkness*. In Conrad's exploration of human nature, however, Kurtz has genuinely debased himself in the absence of the checks and balances of civilization, and he recognizes this in one of the most famous lines in modern literature: "The horror! The horror!"[10] Marlow, moreover, returns to civilized London having discovered his own—and everybody else's—potential to fail, to collapse morally when plunged into the jungle without familiar rules and supports.

Few people today would see Gonzalo's behaviour as moral degradation, and Gonzalo is not known to have uttered any kind of Conradian self-condemnation. For his part, sure in his own faith and morality, Aguilar came away from the encounter with no sense of personal vulnerability. Standing face to face with Gonzalo, he saw only a superficial reflection of himself: he had kept to his prayer book while the other had become a heathen; he had become a humble servant of his *cacique* while the other had become a proud and decorated war captain; and he had remained chaste when presented with great temptation while the other had married a heathen and fathered her children. In his own eyes, and in those of chroniclers to follow, the upright Aguilar was a living rebuke to the fallen Gonzalo.

Whatever he thought of Gonzalo, Aguilar did his best to persuade him to return with him to Cortés. According to Díaz del Castillo, Aguilar reminded him that he was a Christian putting his soul in peril for a native woman, and then he added, surely disingenuously given that Cortés was on a mission of conquest, that he could take his wife and children with him.[11] Undoubtedly, Aguilar would have appealed to his love of country, his culture, his home, and his family back in Palos: was Gonzalo prepared never to see his homeland or loved ones again? Aguilar might even have invoked the glorious crusade on which they had embarked so many years earlier, the building of empire and the saving of souls, and pointed out that everywhere on the peninsula were signs that the golden age of the Maya was in the distant past.

The Maya had arisen out of peoples who had migrated around 2000 BCE to the Yucatán Peninsula from the mainland of what is now Mexico, and over the next two millennia they had developed a highly sophisticated society. Between 250 and 900 CE, their classic period, they built their great cities, created a hieroglyphic writing system, conceived an elaborate cosmology, became skilled astronomers and devised complex calendars that could predict eclipses far into the future, and devised a system of numbers more advanced than that being used in many parts of Europe. The Yucatán was ruled by a series of city-states, each with its own sphere of influence, within which existed a well-developed class system and political hierarchy. For 700 years, it was, in short, one of the most advanced societies in the world.

Then, in one of history's greatest mysteries, the Mayan civilization collapsed, not suddenly but over several hundred years, a decline beginning in the lowlands of what is now Belize and Guatemala and spreading north into the Yucatán. It was implosion rather than destruction by invading forces, and many explanations have been offered for it: climate change, disease, drought, over-population, exhaustion of the soil and depletion of the vegetation, and loss of faith in the theocratic leaders. For whatever reason, the great cities were essentially abandoned; the building of temples, palaces, and monuments ceased; and the once lavish religious ceremonies were reduced to the tribal rituals of jungle dwellers. They were not yet the piles of rubble or reassembled skeletal stone structures that attract the twenty-first-century tourist, but the signs of decay—the smooth stucco crumbling from the walls and walkways and the delicately painted religious and historical images bleaching in the sun—would have been obvious to Gonzalo.

Even more dramatic evidence of the Mayan decline lay much closer to him, in Oxtankah, a sizable city in the southern Yucatán at the heart of the domain of his Chactemal tribe. The stone structures erected between 200 and 600 CE had fallen into disuse and disrepair after the city was abandoned around 900 CE, and when, in the fifteenth century, the Maya had begun to reinhabit it, they had built their homes from stones scavenged from the ruined temples and palaces. Behind the utilitarian needs of the present were the inescapable reminders of a much more magnificent past.

Did Gonzalo want to be on the wrong side of a great struggle? Aguilar might have asked. The answer was that Gonzalo did want to be on that side, and, said his fellow castaway to Cortés, "by no words or admonishments could he be persuaded to come."[12]

⌖⌖⌖⌖⌖⌖⌖⌖⌖⌖⌖⌖⌖⌖⌖

Yucatán historian Inga Clendinnen has pinpointed the challenge lying at the heart of the story of Guerrero and Aguilar: "What it was that held Aguilar to his Spanish and Christian sense of self, yet allowed Guerrero to identify with native ways, is mysterious."[13] Aguilar's behaviour has always been more easily understood—or perhaps more comfortably interpreted—by the Spanish chroniclers and by historians over the years. His tale is one of Christian fortitude and endurance in the face of rigorous captivity. Guerrero's tale is one of a man choosing to abandon his own people and culture and embrace the life of the other.

The immediate response of Guerrero's fellow Spaniards in the New World and the writers who followed later in the sixteenth century was to blacken his character and damn Guerrero. According to the chronicler Francisco López de Gómara, Aguilar ascribed Guerrero's refusal to leave Chactemal to shame, knowing how his tattoos and facial jewellery—and especially his native wife and half-caste children—would be seen by the conquistadors. As much as Guerrero might like to rejoin his fellow Castilians, the mark of the heathen was forever inscribed on his face and inherently in the faces of his wife and children. There was, implied Aguilar, no going back.

In López de Gómara's recounting of this testimony, Aguilar added that Guerrero might have been held back by "attachment to his wife and love of his children."[14] Other early historians adopted the same disparaging approach, going beyond the circumstances of his life in Chactemal to portray him as innately corrupt, lower class, or racially impure. Cervantes de Salazar claimed that the renegade did not accept the invitation of Cortés because of the "vice" that he had committed with a Mayan woman.[15] The chronicler Gonzalo Fernández de Oviedo went further, describing Guerrero as "this evil person, as he must have been from his origins brought up among low and vile people, and one who was not well taught in the elements of our Holy Catholic Faith, or who was...of low race and suspect of not being of the Christian religion."[16]

In this one brief but sweeping comment, Fernández de Oviedo succeeded in damning Guerrero as being flawed in all the important ways that a sixteenth-century Spaniard would have been measured: class, religion, and race. Assumed to have been a sailor from Spain's west coast, he would not have been a gentleman conquistador—that is, from a middle-class or upper-class family—but a common labourer or seaman. His having become an idolater, an inference made easily and quickly by all the chroniclers, was seen as evidence that he did not have a proper Catholic upbringing. Finally, and perhaps most damning of all, Fernández de Oviedo suggests that Guerrero might have been a Muslim or Jew—or devious *converso*—who could thus have easily fallen into another kind of heresy.

Behind the condemnation of the chroniclers lay the political and cultural imperatives of the time: Guerrero's shocking behaviour had to be explained and accounted for in a way that did not threaten the certainty of the Spaniards in their religious and ethnic crusade. In Clendinnen's words, "for one of their own to acquiesce in such filthiness, and to choose it over his own faith and his own people, was to strike at the heart of their sense of self."[17]

Many later historians, however, followed the idea of the weak, flawed man. In the nineteenth century, Washington Irving, the American author of "The Legend of Sleepy Hollow" and "Rip Van Winkle" and of three books of Spanish history, depicted Guerrero as an opportunist who, "being a thorough son of the sea, seasoned to all weathers, and ready for any chance or change,...soon accommodated himself to his new situation." This accommodation, continued

Irving, in the language of both the writer of fiction and a man who shared the racial attitudes of his era, was superficial opportunism, which Guerrero would have abandoned if at all possible:

> His heart...yearned after his native country, and he might have been tempted to leave his honours and dignities, his infidel wife and half savage offspring behind him, but an insuperable, though somewhat ludicrous, obstacle presented itself to his wishes....His face and hands were indelibly painted or tattooed; his ears and lips were slit to admit huge Indian ornaments, and his nose was drawn down almost to his mouth by a massy ring of gold, and a dangling jewel.
>
> Thus curiously garbed and disfigured, the honest seaman felt that, however he might be admired in the Yucatan, he should be apt to have a hooting rabble at his heels in Spain. He made up his mind, therefore, to remain a great man among the savages, rather than run the risk of being shown as a man monster at home.[18]

Historians in our own time, though having shed the patronizing racist attitudes of earlier ages, still suggest that Guerrero's behaviour in captivity was reactive, that it was the response of a man weakened and made vulnerable by the rigours of shipwreck and capture. In her scholarly study of the Spanish conquest of the Yucatán, Clendinnen comments that "we know nothing of how Guerrero's remaking as a Maya came about; whether isolation and despair led to collapse, and then a slow rebuilding, or whether knowledge of many ports (he was thought to be a sailor), an ear quick for foreign sounds, a mind curious for foreign ways allowed an easier transition."[19] Others reiterate Aguilar's reported assumption that shame prevented Guerrero from being repatriated.

No one, of course, can know what motivated such a remarkable reinventing of the man. Having left no memoir or written account himself, and having had only the briefest contact with the world outside his corner of the Yucatán—and that in the form of a short letter—in the years following, Guerrero remains as inscrutable as the enigmatic figures in Conrad's novels. Adding to the mystery is the fact that Guerrero's actions were unique: there is no known case of another Spaniard of that period joining an indigenous people and adopting their customs and beliefs. The answer to the mystery, if it can ever be determined, lies somewhere in the particular circumstances of his life and in his character. But, though it would have distressed Aguilar and the Spanish chroniclers, had they permitted themselves to consider it, his decision to remain among the Maya might have had much to do with the Spanish society and culture that Guerrero knew and the Mayan society and culture that he discovered.

◰◰◰◰◰◰◰◰◰◰◰◰◰◰◰◰◰◰

Aguilar might not have come away from his meeting in Chactemal with any real understanding of Guerrero's decision, but it was clear to him that his companion was immovable. Aguilar made his gruelling way back north to the point where he had been told to rendezvous with Cortés' men, but, to his great distress, they had departed. It was only the flotilla's delay in departing Cozumel that allowed him to reach them, a postponement that the Spanish party attributed to divine intervention.

Crowded around him on a Cozumel beach, Cortés and his captains must have looked on Aguilar with great curiosity and heard his narrative with apprehension. Seven years among the Maya would have made him a figure of suspicion, someone perhaps still loyal to his *cacique* and sent to infiltrate the Spanish flotilla, and they would have sized him up. As well, his stories of castaways being sacrificed and eaten would have sent shivers through men about to embark on a long expedition through the Yucatán and the unexplored lands beyond. Indeed, if the chroniclers are to be believed, stories of cannibalism in the New World travelled back even to Spain, where

Aguilar's mother was said to have gone mad at the suggestion that her son had been cooked and eaten. For the remainder of her life, the sight of any meat being roasted or broiled would cause her to shriek "Woe is me! That is my son and my darling!"[20]

Having listened to Aguilar's tale, Cortés concluded not only that Aguilar was no threat to the expedition but also that he could be very useful to it. The years in captivity had made him familiar with the Mayan language, and the conquistador knew that a good interpreter would be essential in negotiations with tribal chiefs on the way to Méjico, wherever and whatever that might be. Aguilar thus went from being a Mayan slave to being an essential component of one of the greatest conquering marches in history.

Guerrero, on the other hand, though of course he could not have known it, had given up the chance to become one of Cortés' celebrated vanquishers of Montezuma and the vast Aztec Empire. Moreover, according to Aguilar, he had gone dramatically in the opposite direction: he was urging his Mayan masters to resist the invasion of their land, teaching them how to fight the Spanish, and even leading their forces. It had been Guerrero at the head of the native forces that had so effectively repelled Hernández de Córdoba at Cabo Catoche two years earlier. On hearing this, Cortés exclaimed, "I wish I had him in my hands for it will never do to leave him here."[21]

The conquistador's words were prophetic. When Cortés sailed away from Cozumel, he left the enigmatic Guerrero behind in the heart of the jungle, but over the next seventeen years of exploration of the Yucatán the Spanish were to find that this mysterious figure never seemed to be far away. As Clendinnen writes, "in the defeats and baffling reversals they were to suffer through the whole of the wearisome conquest of the peninsula, they were able to identify, wherever they were to occur and however implausibly, the mark of his baffling dark intelligence."[22]

"What Would the Spanish Say Should They See Me in This Guise?"

GONZALO AMONG THE MAYA

W hen confronted by crisis, extreme hardship, physical pain, psychological threat, and death, people often collapse and perish. Some, however, display remarkable and almost inexplicable resilience, and they survive. A few not only survive but even thrive in the hostile environment. In 1512, a party of Spaniards was shipwrecked off the coast of Jamaica, was blown across the Caribbean, and fell into the hands of Mayan tribes in the Yucatán Peninsula. Only two of the twenty castaways survived the days on the water in the relentless sun and the years of captivity by the hostile natives of a strange land. One was a cleric and the other a common sailor.

The Spanish chroniclers, notably Bernal Díaz del Castillo and Francisco Cervantes de Salazar, have recorded Jerónimo de Aguilar's account of his survival. Aguilar endured, he told Hernán Cortés and his rescue party, because he served his Mayan captors

obediently and cheerfully, and he won their admiration by resisting the temptations of the beautiful young women offered to him.
Most importantly, he overcame the despair, depression, and sense
of dislocation that sapped the will to live of so many of his fellows
by strict adherence to his Christian faith. He remained convinced
that God, for whom he was an instrument of some higher purpose, would guide him safely back to his own people.

But what of Gonzalo Guerrero? What gave him the strength to
withstand the rigours of his shipwreck and capture, and what gave
him the will to survive and triumph? Unlike Aguilar, he left no
account of his experience, but we can speculate about what might
have given a young sailor from Palos, toughened by the ordeal of
Darién, the traits necessary to endure. And if, amid the alien deities of his Mayan captors, he retained a belief in his Catholic God,
then for what could he have thought God had preserved him?

Unlike Aguilar and almost all the others in the shipwrecked
party, Gonzalo was accustomed to hard labour. Anyone who had
grown up in the working class of an Andalusian seaport, and
who had laboured aboard the ships plying their trade along the
Iberian and African coasts, would have been physically strong
and resilient. He was hardly a middle-class fortune seeker accustomed to comfort, luxury, and servants to do his heavy labour. If
he needed any further hardening, Gonzalo found it scrambling
on the rigging or hauling sails on the heaving sea between Cadiz
and the Spanish Indies. To have survived the severe hardships of
the Darién settlements, when so many others perished, required
a strong constitution and determined will to live. Thus, when he
staggered ashore along the Yucatán coast, Gonzalo had already
been harshly tested, and few men were better suited to survive the
long ordeal that he was about to face.

Such strengths would soon have become apparent to his Mayan
captors, and they would have made Gonzalo a valuable commodity. Like most early cultures—notably the Egyptians, Greeks, and
Romans—the Mayan communities depended heavily on slavery

to provide essential labour. Slaves became an important economic commodity, being sold and traded up and down the Yucatán coast and into the Gulf of Mexico. They were most commonly acquired in battle, after which the victors would immediately sacrifice the high-ranking captives—hence the early deaths of Juan de Valdivia and three others of the shipwrecked Spaniards—and keep those of lower rank as slaves. Despite being condemned to a life of servitude, prisoners who worked industriously were treated relatively well, though many were ultimately sacrificed on the deaths of their masters or to propitiate the gods during times of drought, famine, or disease.

Gonzalo undoubtedly had a strong back for hauling wood and water and tilling and planting the maize fields, but he possessed two things that made him unusually valuable to the Maya: knowledge of the sea and sailing, and knowledge of the strange bearded men beginning to intrude on their lands. He was one of seven survivors who had escaped from their original captors, and, after falling into the hands of another chiefdom, he was sold to Nachan Ka'an, the *cacique* of Chactemal, located at the southeasternmost corner of the Yucatán Peninsula. As such, Gonzalo had become part of the Maya's most seagoing community, a maritime commercial society not unlike that in which he had grown up in Palos.

The Chactemal community was practically surrounded by water. It was flanked on the east by the Bay of Chetumal, a large, shallow body of water separated from the Caribbean by a long finger of land, the Xcalak Peninsula, and extending into what is now Belize. Through the southern opening of this nearly inland sea, the Maya could paddle their eighty-foot cedar canoes down the coast to what are now Honduras, Nicaragua, and Panama. Through the Boca Bacalar Chico, a narrow channel possibly dug by the Maya, they could cut across the peninsula directly to the Caribbean and go north to Tulum, Xel Ha, and Cozumel.

The mainland on all sides of the Chactemal settlement contained more bodies of water—lakes and rivers—than any other territory in Yucatán. Connected to the Bay of Chetumal are a long sliver of a lagoon now called Laguna Guerrero and a lake named Lago Guerrero. Farther inland is Laguna Bacalar, a lagoon fifty kilometres long and ten kilometres wide, connected to the bay by a network of shallow channels and a stream draining into the Hondo River. Since the Hondo stretches 150 kilometres into the interior and itself drains into the Bay of Chetumal, there was a natural marine route linking the mainland tribes to the communities along the Caribbean coast.

The Chactemal Maya became prosperous traders, moving seashells, cotton, feathers, salt harvested from the shallow lagoons, and cacao, grown nowhere else in Yucatán, inland and up the northern coast. They exchanged these and other goods such as honey, wax, obsidian, and jade in Honduras and Nicaragua for the metals not found anywhere in the Yucatán. Indeed, it was the gold and silver jewellery imported from the south that fired the early Spanish dreams of finding vast amounts of treasure on the peninsula.

Such maritime commerce led one historian of the Maya to call the Chactemal Maya "the Phoenicians of Middle America,"[1] and Guerrero, coming from a similarly rich seagoing tradition, must have felt some kinship with them. The seafarers of Chactemal, however, were also called "the guardians of the sands, the guardians of the seas," because they were the first line of defence of the region against predation by hostile tribes from the Mosquito Coast of Nicaragua and elsewhere.[2] The big trading canoes served equally well as war craft patrolling the mangrove-lined lagoons and open water of the Caribbean shoreline. A practised seaman with experience in combat was thus an invaluable asset to the Chactemal Maya, and Gonzalo soon came to be trusted to lead their maritime defences. His greatest role, however, ultimately became that of captain of the Mayan forces repelling the invasion of the Yucatán by enemies much more familiar to him: his own countrymen, the Spanish.

The survival of Gonzalo, like that of Aguilar, was remarkable, but his rise from slave to respected military captain is much more astonishing. At the beginning, Gonzalo was truly an alien among the Maya, a bearded white man of the sort that they had never seen before, a being who washed up on their shore from a land and a culture whose existence they had never known. If stories of the Spanish presence in the Indies or Darién—particularly its brutal treatment of the natives—had filtered into the Yucatán, he would have begun his enslavement as a deeply suspicious figure, seen to be capable, given the opportunity, of betraying his captors to his compatriots. To become accepted as a tribesman who would marry the *cacique*'s daughter required exceptional tact, resolution, courage, and discipline. Above all, it required great adaptability, and this is what made the experience of Gonzalo so fundamentally different from that of Aguilar.

Because Gonzalo was an exotic captive so unlike the indigenous prisoners taken from other tribes, he was a prize claimed by the *cacique* of the Chactemal community, Nachan Ka'an. Attached to this eminent household, he would first have been employed in heavy labour such as hauling wood and water and tilling fields, simple tasks that, in the absence of a common language, he could be assigned by gestures. Most slaves spent their lives—which for some, unfortunately, were brief—in such service, but Gonzalo still burned with some optimism and ambition, and this made him learn the language of his captors, a difficult task since it bore no resemblance to written or spoken Spanish. As he became more proficient in it, he was given more responsibility and more complex tasks, and he gained the confidence of Nachan Ka'an by fulfilling them capably. Having found his tongue among these strangers, he likely began to tell them of his earlier life and his own people, and one can only begin to imagine what the Chactemal Maya made of his talk of Andalusia, Catholicism, armour and gunpowder, ocean-going sailing ships, horses, wheeled vehicles, and so much else. Most importantly, he gave his captors an essential truth that would remain hidden from the other great Middle American civilization, the Aztecs, until it was too late: the Spanish were not gods but men like themselves.

As Nachan Ka'an's respect for, and trust in, his slave grew, Gonzalo must have been aware that his rise from the lowest social rank to a position of prominence would never have been possible in his native Spain. Coming from a family of sailors in Palos, he might have been able to make some fortune in the New World, but it would not have raised him much above the working class at home. Living with the Maya, he found what centuries later would be called the "American Dream," a meritocracy in which character, skill, and ambition outweighed birthright and class and could raise one from slave to captain. Listening to Aguilar plead with him to join Cortés' men, Gonzalo must have known that he would, at the least, be going from Mayan captain back to Spanish foot soldier.

Among the Maya, Gonzalo earned the respect of far more than the *cacique*; he won the admiration of Nachan Ka'an's daughter, Zazil Há, and nothing marked his assimilation into Mayan life as indelibly as their marriage and the children, the first *mestizos* in Mexican history, that came of it. It is this union, the first true marriage in American history of a European and a native, that is celebrated in statues and paintings all over the Yucatán Peninsula.

The story of Gonzalo Guerrero and the Mayan "princess," Zazil Há, like that of John Smith and Pocahontas, or countless Hollywood films such as *Dances with Wolves*, has been romanticized in numerous accounts, and there is an understandable appeal in imagining a growing attraction between the slave and the chief's daughter. Mayan slaves, though not treated as members of the family, were part of the household, and there would have been ample opportunities for the pair to be together. Perhaps, too, an enraptured Zazil Há sat with her father when Gonzalo told his stories of Castile, his youth, and his experiences in Darién. As the exotic stranger revealed more of his character, and perhaps bared something of his soul, a love might have sprung up between him and the beautiful young woman listening attentively in the background. Zazil Há might have pleaded with her father to be allowed to marry the slave rather than some young Mayan warrior.

The marriage of Zazil Há and Gonzalo, however, was likely much more prosaic. Romantic attraction was not an important part of Mayan marriages, most of which were arranged by parents or professional village matchmakers. Indeed, seeking a mate by oneself without the help of experts was considered improper. Fathers in particular were very careful to find appropriate wives, women from the same social class, for their sons, and the family backgrounds of both bride and groom were important. Family lineage ran through the males, with children being given the surname of the father; in addition to this lineage name, however, they adopted a secondary or "house" name taken from the family name of the mother.

Gonzalo, of course, could bring no Mayan lineage name to the marriage. In this sense, he was classless, and any name that he might be given by the tribe would become that by which his *mestizo* children and their descendants would be known. This was a serious impediment to the marriage of anyone enslaved from a foreign tribe, but Nachan Ka'an overlooked it in giving his blessing to the union of Gonzalo and Zazil Há. As the Spaniard rose in his estimation as a worker, sailor, and warrior, he must have looked increasingly like a man with whom the *cacique* could entrust his daughter. If Gonzalo were of average stature for a Spaniard, then he would have been an imposing figure among Mayan men, whose average height was five feet, one inch, and average weight about 120 pounds. As such, he would have looked like someone with whom a woman could be secure and with whom she could raise a protected family. In any case, Gonzalo rose remarkably from slave to man worthy of marrying into the tribe's highest-ranking family.

Following Mayan tradition, the wedding of Zazil Há and Gonzalo took place at the house of Nachan Ka'an, where a feast had been prepared. Guests—including all the prominent figures in the community—met the couple and mingled with the bride's relatives. When the priest was assured that all parties had been consulted and were satisfied with the arrangements, he conducted a simple ceremony, essentially the giving of Zazil Há to Gonzalo. Following this was the nearly universal ritual of a feast, and the couple were then allowed to consummate their marriage.

Tradition required that a newly married couple live in the bride's father's house for five or six years, during which the husband worked for his father-in-law. Thereafter, if the groom performed his duties satisfactorily, he was allowed to set up his own household; if not, he was driven from the family. Since Gonzalo had already performed much of that service as a slave, and had proven to be an exemplary worker, his probation was relatively brief. Then, with the help of the community, he built his *ná*, the traditional Mayan house.

Following a pattern used for centuries before Gonzalo's arrival—and prevalent even today in the remoter villages of the Yucatán—the *ná* was a small apsidal (i.e., roughly oval) structure with walls of adobe-covered tree branches erected on a stone foundation and covered with a roof thatched with palm leaves. The house generally had two entrances: one facing east and the other west so as to catch the early morning and late afternoon sunlight, and Gonzalo would have had to become accustomed to having no doors in his dwelling, household theft or any other kind of intrusion being considered a grave offence among the community-minded Maya. On the other hand, a sailor from Palos accustomed to the hard deck of a ship would not have found it difficult to sleep on a low stand made of saplings and covered with mats, pulling a cotton mantle over himself for warmth. A single wall running lengthways through the house divided the sleeping quarters from a room with whitewashed and, in the case of high-ranking people, beautifully frescoed walls. This was where guests were entertained and lodged.

Outside their house, Gonzalo and Zazil Há had the traditional small Mayan garden, the *milpa*, where they grew a variety of vegetables: beans, squash, pumpkins, sweet potatoes, sweet and hot peppers, and tomatoes. Fruit trees growing in the *milpa* or nearby jungle provided papaya, custard apple, sapodilla, avocado, and breadnut. Like all other married couples, Gonzalo and Zazil Há were also given a piece of land about 400 square feet on the outskirts of the community; called a *hun uinic*, its primary purpose was cultivation of the crop on which the Mayan civilization was built: maize. This was done by a centuries-old system of slash-and-burn in which a tract of jungle was cut down with a stone axe and then burned, and then seeds were planted in the ash-enriched soil. A crop could be grown successfully for a few seasons before the land was left fallow for eight years and new land had to be cleared.

In his transformation from Spanish sailor to Mayan tribesman, Gonzalo became accustomed to both a new diet and a new way of farming. From the day that Columbus first set foot in the West Indies to Gonzalo's capture along the Yucatán coast, the Spanish had been reluctant to eat the unfamiliar foods of the New World. Only sustained famine, when their European crops failed to flourish in American soil and supply ships from home went astray, made them desperate enough to turn to indigenous vegetables, fruits, and animals. So different were the diets of the Spanish and the natives of the New World that seven years of eating like the Maya had given Aguilar a stomach unaccustomed to staples of the Spanish table. Conversely, some of the others among the shipwrecked party likely died from being unable to adjust to the foods given to them by their Mayan captors.

Most of the staples of the Mayan diet—now common foods in most of the modern world—were strange to Gonzalo and his compatriots. Tomatoes, potatoes, sweet potatoes, squash, pumpkins, sweet and hot peppers, manioc (an edible tuber also known as cassava), papaya, and avocado were unknown in Spain. Cacao, so prized by the Maya that its beans were used as currency, was considered a very nutritional restorative, either combined with chilies and spices in a frothy drink or mixed with ground maize in a porridge-like dish. One of the commonest vegetables on the Mayan table was—and has remained so for centuries—*chaya*, the leaves of a perennial shrub that, when cooked, resemble spinach but when raw or undercooked exude deadly amounts of cyanide. Other exotic foods included jicama (sometimes called the Mexican turnip), the fruit of the *mamey sapote* tree, and breadnut, often cultivated near villages or brought in from southern regions.

The Yucatán Maya called their territory Uluumil Cutz Tetel Ceh, "Land of Turkey and Deer," and Gonzalo would not have found it difficult to swallow the flesh of either common creature or that of the ubiquitous rabbit. Nor would it have seemed strange to eat the peccary, the flesh of which was said to be superior to that of its distant relative, the European pig; or the tapir, a long-snouted creature resembling a hog but actually more closely related to the horse and rhinoceros. Eating monkeys or domesticated dogs might have given him some pause, as it always has for Europeans, and tasting the roasted flesh of the iguana or armadillo would have been a new experience. Manatees, or sea cows, the large herbivorous mammals so numerous in the Bay of Chetumal and the surrounding lagoons, were hunted for their hides—so useful for war shields, canoe hulls, and sandals. They were also a valuable source of meat, a flesh, like that of the various turtles in the local waters, for which Gonzalo would have had to acquire a taste.

Meat was not a major part of the Mayan diet, however, and Gonzalo had to alter the eating habits of his lifetime. For a man who grew up on the Andalusian fare of bread, wine, olives, meat, and fish, the largest adjustment for him was his tribe's dependence on maize, so important that the Maya believed that the gods had created humans out of it. In reality, several millennia before the arrival of the Spanish, Mesoamerican farmers had created maize by domesticating and cross-breeding a variety of grass called *teosinte*, and soon, like rice in the Orient, it had become a staple that sustained the Maya, Aztecs, and other Central American peoples.

Writing in the mid-sixteenth century, Diego de Landa described the role of maize as he saw it in the daily life of the Maya:

> Their principal subsistence is maize of which they make various foods and drinks, and even drinking it as they do, it serves them both as food and drink. The Indian women put the maize to soak one night before in lime and water, and in the morning it is soft and half-cooked, and thus the husk and the stalk are separated from it; and they grind it upon stones, and they give to the workmen and travellers and sailors large balls and loads of the half-ground maize, and this lasts for several months merely becoming sour. And of that they take a lump which they mix in a vase made of the shell of the fruit, which grows on a tree by which God provided them with vessels. And they drink this nutriment and eat the rest, and it is a savory food and of great sustaining power. From the maize which is the finest ground they extract a milk and they thicken it on the fire, and make a sort of porridge for the morning. And they drink it hot and over that which remains from the morning's meal they throw water so as to drink it during the day; for they are not accustomed to drink water alone. They also parch the maize and grind it, and mix it with water, thus making a very refreshing drink, throwing in it a little Indian pepper or cacao.[3]

Historians have expressed doubts about whether the pre-Hispanic Yucatán Maya ate tortillas, but Landa seemed to be describing them when he wrote that the Maya "make good and healthful bread of different kinds, except that it is bad to eat when it is cold, and so the Indian women take a great deal of trouble making it twice a day."[4] Situated near Honduras and Guatemala, where tortillas were common, Gonzalo's tribe might have used them as a staple at every meal. If so, Zazil Há or a servant, like all Mayan women, would have been kept busy at a labour-intensive task since the men customarily ate twenty tortillas at each meal. Additionally, Gonzalo, when he left for the maize field between four and five o'clock in the morning, would have taken a lump of maize dough and, when he was hungry, mixed it with water to produce a nourishing drink. If he remained in the field until mid-afternoon, he would drink this mixture two or three times or consume maize in the form of tamales. The evening meal, eaten at dusk, would include a stew of whatever meat or fish was available, some vegetables, and a basket of tortillas. Several years of this diet might well have persuaded Gonzalo that, as in the Mayan creation legend, he was indeed made of maize.

Becoming accustomed to a strange diet was one step in his becoming a Maya, but there were others, deeply rooted cultural practices so different from anything that he had known. Some were external and cosmetic, others reaching to the heart of who he was as a Spaniard and a Catholic. Superficially, his experience mirrored that of Aguilar; however, whereas the cleric adapted to his circumstances and waited for God to deliver him from his savage captors, Gonzalo embraced Mayan life.

When Aguilar was brought before Cortés on Cozumel Island after seven years of captivity, no one in the Spanish party could distinguish him from his three Mayan companions. At the same moment, leagues to the south, Gonzalo walked among the Chactemal Maya, and only a shrewd and knowledgeable observer would have spotted him as an outsider. Years in the intense tropical sun had burned his skin brown, and the clothes that he was wearing when he landed in Yucatán had long ago rotted. In place of his sailor's trousers, he was now clad in the *ex*, the traditional native breechcloth that the women carefully wove from cotton. This long strip of cloth was wound several times around the waist and then passed between the legs, with each end hanging down at the front and back. Around his shoulders, he wore a garment somewhat like a shawl or poncho, a covering also used for warmth while sleeping, and it was decorated to reflect the rank and esteem that Gonzalo had then achieved in the Chactemal tribe. On his feet, as protection against the jagged Yucatán limestone, he wore the *xanabkeuel*, sandals made from hemp or, more commonly, the hide of a deer or tapir and fastened on the feet by two strips of leather. Like Aguilar, he wore his hair in the Mayan style: singed or cropped short on top but left long on the sides and back so that it could be wrapped around his head, braided, and left hanging down the back like a queue. Following the common practice of Mayan men, he decorated it with a mirror-like fragment of obsidian.

Clothed and styled in such a way, Gonzalo easily blended in with the other men in his tribe, but his foreign origins were betrayed by one bodily characteristic. The indigenous peoples of the New World had little or no facial hair, and beards and moustaches were considered ugly. In fact, facial hair was so disliked by the Maya that mothers burned the faces of their young sons with hot cloths to keep their beards from growing, or they plucked out the hairs one by one in a process that must have seemed like torture. Gonzalo's hirsuteness would not have appealed to Zazil Há, at least initially, and Gonzalo might have shaved with a crude razor fashioned from a fragment of obsidian or endured a long and painful plucking. Years later, however, facial hair would become an essential clue to his ultimate fate.

Had Gonzalo's physical transformation among the Maya ended there, Aguilar would have been neither surprised nor shocked when, carrying the request from Cortés that Gonzalo join his forces, he met him again in 1519. Except perhaps for the socially important decoration of the shoulder cloth, Gonzalo would not then have looked much different from his fellow captive. Unlike Aguilar, however, he had risen to prominence in his Mayan tribe, and his body carried dramatic evidence of how profoundly he had embraced its culture and practices.

Gonzalo wore earrings, but not the relatively modest and discreet ornaments sported by twenty-first-century men of fashion. Mayan earrings were large wooden plugs or other ornaments fashioned from bone, shell, or stone, and since they could be an inch in diameter the men's earlobes had to be prepared from boyhood. A perforation was made, and as the years passed and the youth entered manhood the hole was gradually widened. The accompanying discomfort, endured over the growing years as part of the Mayan manhood ritual, would have been considerable, but one can only imagine the pain that Gonzalo suffered as his fully formed adult ears were punctured severely enough to hold the proper earrings. If, because he rose to a position of prominence in his Mayan community, Gonzalo wore a nose ring, then he would also have withstood the pain of having his nasal septum pierced so that it could carry a wooden plug and, during celebrations and important ceremonies, a gemstone.

The Maya saw a man's ability to endure pain as a sign of valour and strong character, and Gonzalo rose in their esteem with each bodily mutilation that he suffered. Even more visible signs of his courage were the tattoos covering his face, put there by a process both uncomfortable and dangerous to the person's health. "They tattoo their bodies," wrote Landa,

> and are accounted valiant and brave in proportion to its amount, for the process is very painful. In doing it the craftsman first covers the part he wishes with color, and then delicately pierces the pictures in the skin, so that the blood and color leaves the outlines on the body. This they do a little at a time, on account of the pain and because of the disorders that ensue; for the places fester and form matter. But for all this they ridicule those who are not tattooed.[5]

In addition to his tattoos, Gonzalo's body was coloured according to his position in the tribe. If Gonzalo was an unmarried youth, he would have painted his body with black hues; since he was a married warrior, he was stained red, the dye coming from the seeds of the achiote tree, still used today to colour and flavour

Yucatán cuisine. History does not record, however, several other physical alterations that would have made him more fully Maya. A practice more common among the women but still adopted by many men was the filing of teeth to points, a mouth full of saw points being considered aesthetically pleasing. No less painful, though much less apparent to the public eye, was the slicing of the man's foreskin so that the penis came to look as if it was encircled by a tassel.

The Aguilar who stood across from Gonzalo in 1519 had come to him excited by the possibility of their being reunited with their Spanish countrymen, and he had little doubt that he himself could cast off the trappings of his Mayan life and again become a good Christian Spaniard. Looking at the figure before him, however, he must have been equally convinced that returning to his previous life had become impossible for his fellow castaway. Gonzalo had gone far beyond him in his physical transformation, and, much more seriously, he had obviously embraced the Mayan life intellectually and spiritually. Only Gonzalo would ever know the depth and breadth of that embrace—to what degree he had thrown off any vestiges of his Christian faith and Andalusian upbringing—but from this point on Spanish chroniclers saw him as a sinner and an abomination.

One element of Gonzalo's life among the Chactemal Maya that his former countrymen would have found foreign on a cultural level and appalling on a spiritual level was hygiene. The Maya, like the Aztecs, placed a high value on personal cleanliness, a trait that can still be found among their twenty-first-century descendants. The men bathed—usually in a steam bath prepared by the women—every afternoon after coming in from their work in the fields, and some high-ranking members of the communities bathed and changed their garments several times a day. The sixteenth-century Spanish, on the other hand, rarely washed more than their hands, parts of their faces, and their mouths. Religious leaders had decided that public bathing could lead to immorality, promiscuity, and the spread of disease; even complete immersion in private was thought to lead to the contraction of disease because, as the warm water opened the pores of the bather, infection would invade the body. The ordinary Spaniard therefore preferred a lack of hygiene and smelling like a badly kept animal to the risk of catching the plague germ or some other lethal virus. Queen Isabella herself is said to have claimed that she had had only two baths in her life: when she was born and when she was about to be married. And, on hearing Columbus report on the repeated cleansing practised by natives in the Spanish Indies, she issued an edict to prohibit frequent bathing.

If their early sightings of the Spanish—with their large ships, armour, cannons, and dress—suggested to the Maya and Aztecs that they were dealing with sophisticated intruders, their noses would have convinced them otherwise. Weeks of slogging through the Yucatán jungle and fighting native warriors, all the while clad in armour in the tropical heat, made the conquistadors reek. Natives often met them holding flowers to their noses, much like aristocratic Europeans of the time clutched scented handkerchiefs against the odours of their companions. Moreover, during their meetings with the conquistadors, tribal chiefs would ensure that the rooms were filled with the smell of copal, the aromatic tree resin that they called *pom*, burned as incense. The Spanish chroniclers correctly assumed that the Maya used it as a purification ritual, but several recent historians have suggested that it also served well to mask the offensive smell of the strange men sitting across from them.

For the Maya, of course, bathing went beyond mere concern for hygiene; it had, like most of their practices, a religious significance, and it was this that most concerned early Spanish clerics and administrators. Like many of the indigenous peoples of the Americas, the Maya used the sweat lodge for a purification ritual that both cleansed the body of toxins and healed the mind of spiritual anxiety, uncertainty, and ennui. Such bathing was common in ancient Rome, Finland, Russia, Turkey, and Japan, but it was foreign to Spain. It was thus doubly abhorrent to the early Spanish in the Yucatán, and they outlawed its use.

Like the diet, the tattoos, and the body scarification, the sweat lodge was a Mayan practice that would have been a considerable challenge for Gonzalo. The heat during the sweat was so intense that the participant's body temperature often reached 104 degrees Fahrenheit, causing a much faster, more powerful heartbeat believed to release toxins. For anyone unaccustomed to the severity of the heat and the shock of the subsequent cold water dousing, the experience was intense and even hazardous. At least one sixteenth-century chronicler saw the sweat as formidable for an outsider. After sweating thoroughly from heat that is "almost unbearable," he wrote, the natives

> wash themselves with cold water outside the bathhouse so that the fiery bath will not remain in their bones. It frightens one to see someone with an exposed body...having sweated for one hour...receive the splash of ten or twelve pitchers of water, without fear of any harm. Truly this seems brutal, but I understand that the body becomes inured and that he who was brought up in this system finds it natural. If a Spaniard were to go through this, he would go into shock or become paralyzed.[6]

Gonzalo neither lost his senses nor was stricken with paralysis, instead becoming inured physically and accustomed ritually to the bathing practices of his new community. And it was only one of many beliefs and rituals that he had to adopt if he were to be fully accepted by Nachan Ka'an's tribe and if he were to participate in the daily life of the people. Much more than that of the Spanish Catholics of Gonzalo's youth, the life of the Maya was ruled by the gods. "Religion pervaded everything," writes Victor von Hagen. "The whole of Maya life was religiously oriented—birth, death, agriculture, time-count, astronomy and architecture. Life itself was bound up with religion and rituals."[7] "They had such a great quantity of idols," reported Landa,

> that even those of their gods were not enough; for there was not an animal or insect of which they did not make a statue, and they made all these in the image of their gods and goddesses.... The wooden idols were so much esteemed that they were considered as heirlooms and were the most important part of the inherited property.... They knew well that the idols were the works of their hands, dead and without a divine nature; but they held them in reverence on account of what they represented, and because they had made them with so many ceremonies.[8]

No one from Gonzalo's background would have found it unusual to call on a deity to bring one good fortune or good health. The Catholic Church of his youth had God, Christ, and the Virgin Mary as well as a variety of saints—patrons who might intercede on behalf of almost any cause and any person: orphans, merchants, prostitutes, musicians, writers, scholars, and lovers. As a sailor, Gonzalo would have been familiar with Brendan the Navigator and Nicholas of Myra, two of a number of patron saints to whom mariners looked for protection. And, facing the vagaries of the high seas, he would have been as eager as any crewman to beseech God and the Virgin Mary to provide good sailing weather and to protect the ship from disaster.

The Maya, too, looked for supernatural help in facing the difficulties of life, but the gods were a much more pervasive part of their worldview and daily lives. The Mayan religious pantheon contained a multitude of deities: thirteen heavens and nine hells arranged in layers and each presided over by a god, each with its own function, and the Maya looked to them for guidance in even the simplest of tasks. It was important to treat each god with reverence and to offer sacrifices to it in the appropriate manner and at the proper time.

While devout Catholics practised their faith both to ensure a tolerable life on Earth and, more importantly, to prepare their souls for a suitable afterlife, the Maya worshipped their gods primarily to secure the necessities of their earthly lives: fertility, good health, and sustenance. They interpreted the absence of these essentials—in times of pestilence, war and social dissension, or drought and crop failure—as signs of anger in the gods, wrath that had to be appeased by ritual offerings and sacrifices.

Gonzalo would have observed the roles of deities in Mayan daily life when he planted his first field of maize. Following the practice of his fellow farmers, he paid tribute, through a small carving or other gift, to Yum Kaax, a figure frequently portrayed as a young man holding an ear of maize. The god of wild vegetation and the protector of wild animals, he had the power to protect crops from the destructive incursion of the jungle, over which he had control. So important to the Maya was Yum Kaax that he eventually became known as the god of maize.

Even more important to the Maya was Chac, the rain god without whose blessing no crops would grow. Farmers the world over have always looked anxiously to the skies for rain, but the Yucatán Maya were more than usually dependent on the elements: they planted their crops on the thinnest of soil layers through which water quickly percolated through the underlying limestone into underground reservoirs. Hence the primacy of Chac, the god whose intervention was sought by the Maya more often than that of any other deity: in the three codices that survived the Spanish burning of the Mayan written records, he is represented 218 times, while the chief god, Itzamna, is portrayed only 103 times.

Chac was both a singular deity and a multiple one, there actually being four Chacs, each one associated with one of the cardinal points of the compass. In the unified form, he was represented as having fish scales, a curled nose, and a protruding lower lip;

he is also portrayed as carrying axes and snakes with which he strikes clouds to produce rain. Since he could also deliver devastating hailstorms and hurricanes, common events in the Yucatán, he needed to be entreated and soothed, and this was done in elaborate ceremonies performed annually both in the fields and in the public areas of the villages.

Gonzalo would have encountered—and accepted—another important Mayan deity in his own house. Early in their marriage, Zazil Há, following the practice of generations of Mayan women, would have placed a strange idol under her bed, a holy object carved in the shape of an old woman with a headdress made of snakes and having jaguar claws instead of hands. This was Ix Chel, the consort of Itzamna in the Mayan religious pantheon, worshipped in part as the goddess of weaving but much more importantly as a goddess of fertility. A woman favoured by her could expect to become pregnant and be protected through the difficulties of childbirth.

So important was Ix Chel that a shrine dedicated to her on Cozumel Island became the most important pilgrimage site on the Yucatán Peninsula, second only to the sacred *cenote* at Chichén Itzá. Zazil Há likely joined the stream of women who trekked on narrow jungle trails from remote villages to cross the Cozumel strait to pay homage to the goddess. It is likely that Gonzalo commanded the party that took her on the long journey across the Bay of Chetumal, through the narrow Boca Bacalar Chico channel across the Xcalak Peninsula, up the coast past Tulum, and across the nineteen kilometres of treacherous water to Cozumel. We can only imagine the thoughts that went through his mind as he waited while she offered her gifts and prayers to the deity variously known as the Moon Goddess and Lady Rainbow.

And, in the absence of any account from Gonzalo himself, we can only speculate about what might have gone on in his mind, the first real site in history where Mayan religious beliefs confronted Catholicism. Was Gonzalo really the anti-Aguilar, the apostate who completely cast off the faith of his own people, as one would throw off an unwanted cloak, and fully embraced the ancient beliefs of the New World? Or did he publicly perform the rituals of daily life while privately, even in the sequestered conversations of his own consciousness, keep a core of Christian belief alive within him?

Or did Zazil Há, with the blessing of Nachan Ka'an, allow some vestiges of Catholicism—perhaps a crucifix that Gonzalo had carved from the prized Chactemal redwood—in their home? Did she go further and permit her husband to teach their children about his own religious beliefs, as long as such knowledge did not threaten their faith in the traditional gods of her people? Could there have been a blending of faiths, the wooden cross being seen as a form of the Mayan sacred *ceiba* tree and the Virgin Mary another guise of Ix Chel?

If there was a merging of faiths in the household of Zazil Há and Gonzalo, then it was a paradigm for the next 500 years of religious history in the Yucatán. The first century of Spanish occupation was one of brutal suppression, indeed attempted extinction, of the traditional faiths of the Maya and, farther west, the Aztecs. On the surface, this campaign was remarkably successful as temples were torn down and the stones used to build chapels and cathedrals, relics destroyed and replaced by Catholic symbols, and native priesthoods disbanded and replaced by increasing numbers of Spanish clergy. Within a generation, the indigenous population of Mexico had largely been baptized and become practising Catholics.

The Catholicism observed by the Maya, however, was hardly that which had been brought across the Atlantic by the Spanish clerics. Accepting the deities and rituals imposed on them by the invaders did not mean abandoning the cosmology of thousands of years; instead, the Maya created a form of syncretism, merging Catholic rituals with traditional native ceremonies. Thus, for example, the Christian resurrection story became associated with the maize god's narrative of sacrifice and rebirth; All Saints' Day and All Souls' Day became merged with the indigenous Day of the Dead observances; and the religious calendar was reconfigured to include both Catholic holidays and those that honoured the many Mayan deities of the landscape, vegetation, and animal life. As late as the nineteenth-century Caste War in the Yucatán Peninsula, the ancient Mayan tradition of oracular shrines was adapted to the central Christian symbol with the famous Talking Cross of Chan Santa Cruz (now the town of Felipe Carillo Puerto). For a number of years, Maya seeking to regain control of their traditional land were inspired by a cross that spoke to them in their own tongue, a miracle cleverly produced by the ventriloquism of a priest hidden in a compartment near the icon. Even the twenty-first-century faith of much of the Yucatán can best be described as a Mayan religion overlaid by a Catholic veneer.

Given this long history of religious syncretism in the Yucatán, it would not be surprising if a form of it developed in the household of Zazil Há and Gonzalo, one in which the Spaniard performed the rituals of the dominant faith while retaining some essential elements of his own native belief. If he had left Spain as a staunch believer in Catholicism, then concern for the salvation of his soul would have demanded as much. That concern, moreover, would surely have extended to the souls of his children, and it might have been in them that the fusion of faiths really occurred.

The little that is known about the children—Aguilar's report to Cortés that Gonzalo had expressed pride in his "handsome" boys—suggests that they were not brought up entirely according to traditional Mayan customs. Gonzalo would scarcely have shown them with pleasure to his fellow Spaniard if, for example, they had the flattened heads considered attractive among the Maya, particularly high-ranking ones. This appearance was created by a procedure, begun five days after birth, in which the baby's head was bound between two boards, one pressing on the forehead and the other on the back of the skull. Several months of this pressure produced a permanent sloping forehead and elongated skull, similar to traditional images of the maize god and considered a mark of the ruling class. To add to this appearance of distinction, many children were also given a permanent squint, a cross-eyed look, by hanging a little ball of resin or wax in front of their eyes. And many young Maya walked on permanently bowed legs as a result of being carried according to the traditional Mayan practice of *hetzmek*: that is, carried astride the mother's hip. To Aguilar, children with these characteristics were an abomination, more so if they were the offspring of a Spanish man, but he reported no such malformations in Gonzalo's sons and daughter.

Gonzalo could have helped to mould his children's immediate future by preventing the reshaping of their bodies, but he must have wondered what would eventually become of them—the first mixed-blood people in this new land. They were Maya, and, even to a Spaniard sitting in an isolated village in southern Yucatán, it must have been apparent that history was against them. Gonzalo had seen the imposing seaside city of Tulum, the extensive inland site of Cobá, the great pilgrimage destination of Chichén Itzá, perhaps also Uxmal and Mayapán, and other centres of Mayan life and culture on the peninsula. Wandering through any of these sites would have told him, if Nachan Ka'an and Zazil Há had not, that the golden age of the Maya was buried in the distant past.

Against the recognition that he had become part of a people in decline would have been the certainty that the Spanish were coming. Gonzalo had grown up in Palos against the background of the unification of Aragon and Castile and the creation of a Spain that soon rid itself of the other: Jews and Muslims. He knew of the growing Portuguese Empire in North Africa, and he had seen first-hand the brown-skinned Tainos led through the streets in chains by Columbus. He had heard the stories of the Spanish, having been given the New World for their own by Pope Alexander VI, sweeping through the Caribbean, island by island, until it truly could be called the Spanish Indies. Gonzalo himself had joined the rush to the New World, and in Hispaniola and then Darién he had seen the ruthlessness with which his countrymen subdued the indigenous peoples and planted the flag of Isabella and Ferdinand over more and more of the world. By the time that he had sailed for the Spanish Indies, Spain had become the most powerful country in Europe, and there was nothing that could stop the expansion of its empire. If he needed any reminder of the insatiable Spanish desire for the riches of the New World and the souls of its people, it came five years after his capture, in 1517, when Hernández de Córdoba's expedition landed at Cabo Catoche, on the northeast coast of Yucatán, and when his men fought with Mayan warriors at Champotón on the Gulf of Mexico. Within a year, another small fleet headed by Grijalva was spotted off the coast at Tulum and Xel Ha and then again at Champotón. By the time that word came to Gonzalo in February 1519 that Cortés was situated on Cozumel, he would have known that the Spanish were casting voracious eyes over Yucatán.

Gonzalo was a warrior, a captain in fact, in the Chactemal tribe, and he was familiar with the fighting qualities of the Maya, tough, indomitable men adept at jungle warfare. But he had to know that obsidian spears and axes, bows and arrows, and leather shields would ultimately be no match for the superior weapons of the Spanish: gunpowder, steel, horses, and mastiffs. The Maya could wage a vigorous guerrilla war, one that might keep the invaders at bay for years, perhaps decades (even Gonzalo's lifetime), but they would eventually become enslaved or possibly exterminated.

These thoughts must have passed through his mind as Gonzalo stood before Aguilar. He could accept the offer from Cortés, rejoin the conquistadors, and become part of the Spanish mastery of the New World, an ever-expanding empire that had been celebrated since his childhood. Zazil Há and his children could not have joined him on the Cortés expedition, and he would never have been permitted to bring them into any Spanish colony without their first being christened and given Spanish names. Gonzalo himself had become too deeply Mayan both outwardly and inwardly to be able to return to his Spanish roots. In any case, though he had become one of the other through no choice of his own, he now chose to remain one of them, and he bade farewell to Aguilar.

"Language Is the Perfect Instrument of Empire":
AGUILAR AND THE CONQUEST OF THE AZTECS

When Hernán Cortés was told that Gonzalo Guerrero had chosen to remain with his Mayan family and tribe rather than repatriate himself with his native countrymen, he observed that "I wish I had him in my hands for it will never do to leave him here." This comment might have been impelled by concern for Gonzalo's well-being or empathy for a fellow Spaniard and Catholic entrapped in the dark world of the other, in a land of pagan beliefs and savage customs. It might have been an expression of the conquistador's fear that a Spaniard could become a valuable resource for hostile natives, and, indeed, subsequent events in Yucatán made this remark prophetic. It might also have voiced regret over the loss of someone who might have been invaluable in the ambitious plans of Cortés for the exploration and conquest of Yucatán and the lands beyond.

With Gonzalo in his company, Cortés would have had a man who had lived for seven years among a people about whom the

Spanish knew very little. In the twenty-six years since they had reached the New World, the Spanish had spread throughout the Caribbean and subjugated a variety of ethnic groups; none, however, was part of a civilization as advanced as the Maya, whose elaborate stone buildings had astonished the earliest conquistadors as they approached the shores of Yucatán, or the Aztecs, whose great city, Tenochtitlán, and political power they would discover when they moved into the interior of central Mexico. Because he had been so fully integrated into Mayan tribal life—more completely than any reconnaissance agent could have infiltrated it—Gonzalo could have told Cortés much about the natives: their political and social structures, their religious and cultural attitudes and practices, and especially their methods of warfare. Such information would have provided a valuable context for any interaction with the indigenous people, giving Cortés an advantage over them in any negotiation and smoothing the way to their subjugation.

But it was precisely because Gonzalo had become so deeply immersed in Mayan life that he could not—or would not—join Cortés and become a Spaniard once more. Jerónimo de Aguilar, on the other hand, had fought strenuously to remain firmly grounded as a Spaniard and Catholic and had not been subsumed in the culture of his captors. This made him less useful as a cultural and ethnic resource for Cortés, and Aguilar is reported to have told the conquistador that his knowledge of life in Yucatán was limited to the immediate circumstances of his captivity. Nonetheless, Aguilar retained one immensely valuable asset from his seven years among the Maya—the ability to understand and speak the language of many of them—and this was to make him one of the most important elements in the remarkable conquest of Mexico by Cortés. Indeed, many historians are convinced that Cortés would not have been able to conquer Montezuma and his Aztec Empire without a capable interpreter.

In 1492, a Spanish man of letters, Elio Antonio de Nebrija, published *Gramática Castellana*, one of the first grammars of a modern European language. On being presented with a copy, Queen Isabella inquired about the usefulness of such a volume, and the Bishop of Ávila replied, "Your Majesty, language is the perfect instrument of empire."[1] He was referring primarily, of course, to the importance of linguistic control of conquered peoples, implying that a single standard language could create political cohesion throughout an otherwise ethnically diverse region. The emergence of a vital and vigorous Castilian language at the end of the sixteenth century, one that became linguistically dominant over the southern Iberian Peninsula, was indeed an important factor in the creation of a united Spain. And, as soon as the Spanish crossed the Atlantic, they identified more and more of the New World as theirs through naming: the Mayan cities of T'hó and Zaci became Mérida and Valladolid, the Aztec town of Nochistlán became Guadalajara, and names such as San Miguel, Lima, San Mateo, Vera Cruz, Hispaniola, and Santiago began to be attached to sites throughout North and South America. To effect an even more complete erosion of the identities and self-images of the indigenous peoples of these lands, the Spanish required that their baptisms into the Catholic Church be accompanied by the imposition of Spanish names. This was particularly important in the case of women since many of them became the concubines of the conquistadors, so thousands of Isabelas, Franciscas, Angelinas, Catalinas, Leonoras, Ineses, and more sprang up in the Mayan, Aztec, and Incan populations.

Language played an even more important part in the symbolic acts by which the conquistadors claimed their newly discovered territories on behalf of the Spanish crown. In their early explorations of the New World, these gestures of ownership had included cutting down a tree, erecting a small building, raising a cross, setting a stone cairn or pillar, or clearing a piece of grass. Beginning in 1514, however, the Spanish signified their appropriation of lands with a formal verbal declaration called the *Requerimiento* ("Requisition"), a document that would be read to the natives three times in the presence of the king's notary, who would make a legal record of the occasion. A lack of protest by the indigenous population was interpreted as an agreement to cede their lands and their authority to the Spanish.

The *Requerimiento* began with a brief history of the world, beginning with the creation by "our Lord God Eternal" of the universe and of the first man and woman on the Earth. Although humankind spread throughout the world and became Christians, Jews, and Muslims—and by implication Maya, Aztecs, Incas, and others—God chose Saint Peter to rule them all from his seat in Rome. He and his successors were named "pope," which meant "admirable and greatest father, governor of all men," and one of the most recent of these universal governors had given all of the islands and the mainland of the Ocean Sea (i.e., all of the New World) to the rulers of Spain. Therefore, the document said, it was incumbent on the native population to understand the text, to deliberate on it, and to accept the Catholic Church and its pope as the rulers of the universe and the Spanish king and queen as the monarchs of this newly found land.[2]

The *Requerimiento* concluded with a statement that began with a promise of paternal benevolence but ended with a vicious threat:

> You owe compliance as a duty to the King and we in his name will receive you with love and charity, respecting your freedom and that of your wives and sons and your rights of possession, and we shall not compel you to baptism unless you, informed of the Truth, wish to convert to our holy Catholic Faith as almost all your neighbors have done in other islands, in exchange for which Their Highnesses bestow many privileges and exemptions upon you. Should you fail to comply, or delay maliciously in doing so, we assure you that with the help of God we shall use force against you, declaring war upon you from all sides and with all possible means, and we shall bind you to the yoke of the

Church and of Their Highnesses; we shall enslave your persons, wives, and sons, sell you or dispose of you as the King sees fit; we shall seize your possessions and harm you as much as we can as disobedient and resisting vassals. And we declare you guilty of resulting deaths and injuries, exempting Their Highnesses of such guilt as well as ourselves and the gentlemen who accompany us. We hereby request that legal signatures be affixed to this text and pray those present to bear witness for us, etc.[3]

As Stephen Greenblatt has observed, the *Requerimiento* was "a strange blend of ritual, cynicism, legal fiction, and perverse idealism."[4] Writing in the middle of the sixteenth century, Bartolomé de Las Casas commented that he did not "know whether to laugh or cry at the absurdity"[5] of its premises, and two native chiefs in Central America responded to an explanation of the *Requerimiento* by declaring that the pope must have been drunk when he gave the Spanish monarchs so much of the world inhabited by others.

The true absurdity of the *Requerimiento* lay in the assumption that indigenous peoples in the Caribbean, on the mainland of Mexico, and in the mountains of Peru could respond at all meaningfully to a document in a language that they could not understand. Its creators had directed that every effort should be made to ensure that the subjugated populations comprehended the terms of the document and the legal force of its reading, but this required capable translators, whom the Spanish expeditions rarely had. Thus, few of the native listeners who gathered on the beaches, in forest clearings, or in village meeting places had any idea what the Spanish were proclaiming. Nor did it help when the Spanish, as the Grijalva expedition did on Cozumel, stuck a copy of the *Requerimiento* on the wall of a shrine to be perused by any of the many Maya who missed the reading. For the conquistadors, the mere ceremonial reading of the *Requerimiento* gave legitimacy to their annexation of foreign territories, a practice seemingly based upon the belief that there was no real language barrier between the indigenous peoples and the Spanish. However, while the conquistadors would have had some familiarity with other European languages, such as Portuguese, Italian, French, and English, related languages in which concepts can be communicated fairly easily, they would not have understood how truly foreign in vocabulary, grammar, structure, and worldview Mesoamerican languages were.

While the legal authorities of the royal court in Castile could afford to be blind to the lack of communication between their colonizing forces and native populations, those in the field in the New World could not. Translation, as Camilla Townsend points out, was essential:

> If they wanted to extend Spain's dominion—and Cortés explicitly did—then a translator had to be present to convey the meaning of the military victory, the new set of expectations, to those who had been conquered. These early translators had to be liminal people, figures who had lived in both worlds, in order to be truly effective. They had to be one of "us people here," and yet not. Children who had been kidnapped and forced to live with the Spanish for years were perfect.[6]

Almost as perfect a translator was a Spaniard like Aguilar who had been captured and forced to live among the Maya for many years.

The first attempts of the Spanish to use native translators in their exploration of the Yucatán Peninsula were far from satisfactory. In one of his forays ashore in his 1517 exploration, Hernández de Córdoba captured two native men, both cross-eyed in the Mayan style, named them Melchorejo and Julianillo, and took them back to Cuba to learn Spanish. Julianillo returned to Yucatán as a translator with the Grijalva expedition the next year, but died soon after, so it was left to Melchorejo to accompany Cortés in 1519.

Julianillo and Melchorejo were barely serviceable as translators, the former suffering from bouts of depression at being abducted from his community and home, the latter being an ordinary fisherman who appeared to have limited ability even in his own language. Moreover, the pair presented the problem that confronts all invading forces that rely on translators and interpreters plucked from among the people being invaded: how does one know that they are honest and loyal? How can one be sure that the communications with the other side, the conversations back and forth, are being conveyed accurately and that the translator or interpreter is not feeding vital tactical information to the enemy? Such doubts came to the fore, in fact, early in the Cortés expedition when Melchorejo fled one night in a canoe, leaving behind his Spanish clothes hung up on a palm tree just as he left behind any loyalty that he might have had to the Spanish. And, as Cortés feared, he proceeded to brief the native chiefs on the Spanish strengths and weaknesses, reporting that the invaders were relatively few in number and could be beaten by sustained assaults.

In the absence of capable and trustworthy translators, Aguilar was a godsend to Cortés. Having kept his identity as a Castilian firmly grounded during his captivity by the Maya, he could be trusted to remain loyal and to convey his commander's words accurately without adding any counterproductive observations. Most importantly, he could be trusted not to reveal any of the duplicity, schemes, traps, or tricks that might lie behind the offers and guarantees of Cortés. As well, his religious training meant that Aguilar could explain the intricacies of Catholic belief and ritual to potential native converts, and Cortés was driven by a near-fanatical desire to replace the pagan beliefs of the New World with the Christian beliefs of the Old World. And, unlike Julianillo or Melchorejo, Aguilar could speak with some authority to them about the political structures that had sent these forces across the ocean and into their lands.

Of all the names of eminent figures in Bernal Díaz del Castillo's great chronicle, *The Discovery and Conquest of Mexico: 1517–1521*, few appear more often than that of Aguilar. Díaz del Castillo refers to the Spanish party's "good fortune to carry such a useful and faithful interpreter along with us,"[7] and it is clear from his account that, from the time Aguilar joined the forces of Cortés on Cozumel Island until the defeat of the Aztecs at Tenochtitlán, he was at the focal point of almost every interaction among the Spanish commander, his captains, and the peoples whom they met. Standing on the deck of the command ship talking to warriors in war canoes, or sitting in the aromatic copal smoke of a council with native chiefs, Aguilar became the mouthpiece of Cortés.

It was a role that Aguilar accepted with relish and one that he filled with more than mere linguistic skill. When the occasion required it, he dramatized the diplomatic approaches of Cortés, providing the tone of both the velvet glove and the mailed fist. Following the first battle with Mayan warriors in Tabasco in March 1519, for example, Aguilar addressed two prisoners who were to take an offer of apparent conciliation back to their chiefs:

> These two messengers were given green and blue beads, and Aguilar spoke many pleasant and flattering words to them, telling them that they had nothing to fear as we wished to treat them like brothers, that it was their own fault that they made war on us, and that now they had better collect all the Caciques of the different towns as we wished to talk to them, and he gave them much other advice in a gentle way so as to gain their good will. The messengers went off willingly and spoke to the Caciques and chief men, and told them all we wished them to know about our desire for peace.[8]

When the *caciques* had considered the message from Cortés, they sent fifteen of their slaves back with gifts of food but also with the painted faces of Mayan warriors:

When these men came before Cortés he received them graciously, but Aguilar the interpreter asked them rather angrily why they had come with their faces in that state, that it looked more as though they had come to fight than to treat for peace; and he told them to go back to the Caciques and inform them, that if they wished for peace in the way we offered it, chieftains should come and treat for it, as was always the custom, and that they should not send slaves. But even these painted faced slaves were treated with consideration by us and blue beads were sent by them in [a] sign of peace, and to soothe their feelings.[9]

Several days later forty regally dressed *caciques* arrived asking for forgiveness for their past warlike behaviour and promising friendship, but they were again greeted by a seemingly angry conquistador and his interpreter:

Cortés, through Aguilar the Interpreter, answered them in a rather grave manner, as though he were angry, that they well knew how many times he had asked them to maintain peace, that the fault was theirs, and that now they deserved to be put to death, they and all the people of their towns, but that as we were the vassals of a great King and Lord named the Emperor Don Carlos, who had sent us to these countries, and ordered us to help and favour those who would enter his royal service, that if they were now as well disposed as they said they were, that we would take this course.[10]

If, however, they did not yield to the rule of the foreign emperor, Aguilar told the *caciques*, then the Spanish artillery pieces, which the natives believed were malevolent creatures with wills of their own, would destroy them. At this point, as Cortés had planned, a match was secretly put to a large cannon, and the explosion was frightening in the ears of people who knew nothing of gunpowder.

This ruse gave Aguilar the opportunity to assure the *caciques* that his commander had given orders that no harm should come to them.

Even then the Spanish had another trick that played on the Maya's lack of knowledge of things European. Knowing that the natives were terrified of the Spaniards' horses, seeing the animals as having the same independent malicious wills as the cannons, Cortés had arranged to have a particularly powerful stallion brought and tied up in a nearby area that had recently housed a mare in heat. When the stallion caught the scent of the mare, it began to whinny and paw the ground in fierce excitement, all the while looking at the *caciques*, who became convinced that it meant to attack them. When Cortés was certain that they were sufficiently terrified, he rose from his chair, went to the horse, and ordered it to be led away. Aguilar then explained that his leader had told the beast not to be angry because the *caciques* were friendly and wished to make peace. The next day the chiefs returned with gifts of jewellery, quilted cloth, and slaves.

On more than one occasion, Aguilar offered advice to Cortés and even functioned as a kind of negotiator between his leader and the natives. Within only a few days of being ransomed and before the Spanish ships left Cozumel, he advised the local *caciques* to ask Cortés for a letter of recommendation that testified to their cooperation with him. He then persuaded Cortés to provide the letter so that subsequent Spanish expeditions would treat the natives more generously than was their usual practice, a gesture that ensured cooperation from the Cozumel Maya long before the rest of Yucatán was subjugated. On another occasion, Aguilar's knowledge of local practices helped to prevent Spanish hopes from being unnecessarily inflamed. Camped outside Cempoala, near the present city of Vera Cruz, Cortés was informed by breathless and excited advance scouts that, like the legends they had heard of rivers of pearls and fields of gold, the walls of all the houses in the town's central plaza were made of silver. Before the inevitable stampede toward the riches could ensue, however, Aguilar pointed out that it was the practice in that part of the world for houses to be stuccoed with plaster or lime and whitewashed, which would give the effect of burnished silver in the bright tropical sun.

A few days later Aguilar offered Cortés further practical advice as the conquistadors, who had brought only half a dozen slaves with them from Cuba, faced the 250-mile march inland to Tenochtitlán carrying fifty-pound loads on their backs. The custom of the region, said Aguilar, was that in times of peace between tribes a local *cacique* was expected to provide *tamenes*—"porters" or "carriers"—for travellers passing through his territory. Cortés reminded the chiefs of this practice, and on the morning of his departure from Cempoala he had 400 native *tamenes* to do the heavy carrying. From that point until their arrival in the Aztec capital, the Spanish did not have to carry their armour and supplies over the rugged and difficult trails of three mountain ranges on the Mexican mainland.

When Montezuma heard of the arrival of the strangely clad and remarkably armed foreigners on the coast of the Gulf of Mexico, he sent several envoys to sound out their intentions. With these agents came skilled painters to provide the emperor with images of the important components of the invading force: its leader, his captains, the ships, sails, horses, cannons, and his interpreter. Within seven months, Montezuma saw Aguilar face to face when the Spanish entered Tenochtitlán, and the Aztec emperor began negotiations with their commander, meetings that culminated in one of the most important episodes in the conquest of Mexico.

On their arrival in Tenochtitlán on November 8, 1519, an event treated with great ceremony by both hosts and visitors, the Spanish were housed at a palace a few hundred yards from Montezuma's own large and luxurious quarters. This arrangement lasted for some months, during which the emperor's people lavished gifts and food on their guests, until the Spanish began to detect a cooling in the attitudes of their hosts. Two of the natives of Tlaxcala, which had allied itself with the Spanish party on its march across the mainland, conferred secretly with Aguilar, advising him that the Aztecs had become increasingly hostile. This intelligence, combined with word that seven of his men had been killed back at the coast by natives loyal to Montezuma, convinced Cortés to make a pre-emptive strike and take the emperor prisoner. With six of his men and two interpreters, one of whom was Aguilar, Cortés went to Montezuma, complained of the attacks against his forces, and then gave him a brutal ultimatum:

I do not wish to begin a war on this account nor to destroy this city, I am willing to forgive it all, if silently and without raising any disturbance you will come with us to our quarters, where you will be as well served and attended to as though you were in your own house, but if you cry out or make any disturbance you will immediately be killed by these my Captains, whom I brought solely for this purpose.[11]

With justifiable misgivings, Montezuma agreed to accompany the Spanish to their quarters, making himself a hostage and essentially surrendering control of his empire to Cortés. Along with his physical confinement came the equally important destruction of his self-confidence, his belief in his own omnipotence, and his people's faith in his judgment. For ten days, he was allowed the face-saving pretence of having voluntarily joined the Spanish as their guest, but then he was taken to a plaza in front of his palace to watch seventeen of his men, those accused of killing the Spaniards at the coast, burned alive on a pyre made of captured Aztec weapons. To add to his humiliation, Cortés publicly shackled and chained him, an insult so great that some of Montezuma's attendants put their fingers inside the shackles so that the iron would not touch his royal person. A few months later, his spirit broken, Montezuma was dead, either as a result of wounds inflicted by stone-throwing mobs of his own people or at the hands of his Spanish captors, depending on whether one is reading the indigenous accounts or those of the Spanish chroniclers. Little more than a year later the

Aztec Empire fell to Cortés, and the Spanish were in control of Mexico and its riches.

Aguilar's fortunes had undergone a remarkable transformation in the fifteen months from the time of his farewell to Gonzalo and his rescue by Cortés to the destruction of Montezuma. From immersion in the culture and religion of the Maya, among whom, like Gonzalo, Aguilar had survived and, even as a slave, earned the respect of his captors, he had regained his Spanish voice, grown rusty over the seven years of disuse, and had easily recovered the identity of a conquering crusader. And, except for his initial concern for the well-being of the Maya left behind on Cozumel, he apparently had little sympathy for the natives whom Cortés exploited and brutalized on his march to Tenochtitlán. While Gonzalo was continuing his chosen life among the Chactemal Maya as the husband of an indigenous woman, the father of her children, and a respecter of her gods, Aguilar was becoming a conquistador. And with that role came a complete embrace of practices intended to eradicate much of the culture and all of the religion of the New World.

When Cortés set sail from Cuba for Yucatán, he was driven by a number of ambitions: the glory of the discovery of new lands, the acquisition of great wealth, and the spread of Catholicism. Planting the Christian cross in new soil might have been merely a convenient moral justification for invading foreign territories and looting them of riches, but Cortés was determined to destroy any pagan religions in his path. It was a struggle, according to the conquistador's early biographer, Francisco López de Gómara, that began on Cozumel shortly after Aguilar had been ransomed. Cortés told an assembly about the Catholic faith, the one God, and veneration of the cross and Virgin Mary. He condemned the Mayan practice of human sacrifice and described Mayan religious idols as evil. It was a speech delivered as if to persuade its listeners, but, as López de Gómara admitted, the power to convert the natives really lay in the sword:

Truth to tell, it is war and warriors that really persuade the Indians to give up their idols, their bestial rites, and their abominable bloody sacrifices and the eating of men,...and it is thus that of their own free will and consent they more quickly receive, listen to, and believe our preachers, and accept the Gospel and baptism, which is what Christianity and faith consist of.

One of those preachers was Aguilar:

So, Jerónimo de Aguilar preached to them about salvation, and, either because of what he told them, or because of the beginning that they had already made, they were pleased to have their idols cast down, and they even assisted at it, breaking into small pieces what they had formerly held sacred. And soon our Spaniards had left not a whole idol standing.[12]

Thus began the long, dedicated, and extensive Spanish effort to wipe out the indigenous religions of Mexico, a campaign that would be conducted by force and torture, one that would lead, in 1562, to Bishop Diego de Landa's infamous burning of twenty-seven codices, hieroglyphic rolls on which much of Mayan history had been recorded. Only three codices survived to provide some insight into the history of one of the world's great civilizations.

Several weeks after the departure of the Cortés expedition from Cozumel, it made a further assault on Mayan religious belief at Tabasco. After the *Requerimiento* had been read to an assembly of native warriors, and Aguilar had asked for safe passage for the Spanish to collect fresh water, a battle broke out. When the enemy retreated, Cortés emphasized his formal possession of the land by drawing his sword and making three cuts in a large *ceiba* tree growing in the central square of a village. Standing before the tree, he declared that he would defend with his sword the right to make such a gesture.

In cutting into the *ceiba*, a choice perhaps suggested by Aguilar, Cortés was not merely carving a tree but also striking at one of the most important elements of Mayan belief. The *ceiba* was revered because it was seen as the connection between the mysterious underworld and the sky above. Even more dramatic was his gesture several days later when, following sermons on the virtue of Christianity and the iniquity of Mayan beliefs, he had a cross cut deeply into a massive *ceiba* in the town of Cintla. As the years passed and the bark grew around it, the Christian symbol remained overlaid on the Mayan icon.

Little of the history of the Spanish conquest of Mexico has been told from the points of view of Mayan and Aztec chroniclers of the period, but even in the narratives of Spaniards such as Díaz del Castillo and López de Gómara there is evidence that the imposition of Christianity and the attempted expunging of indigenous faiths were very distressing to the natives. At Cempoala, where the Spanish entered the lands ruled by Montezuma, the call to abandon their beliefs and idols was met with protests—and logic—from native leaders. "All the caciques, priests and chiefs," wrote Díaz del Castillo, "replied that it did not seem to them good to give up their idols and sacrifices and that these gods of theirs gave them health and good harvests and everything of which they had need." When Cortés replied that he would accept nothing less than the destruction of all of their religious objects, the "chieftains were beside themselves with fury and called out to Cortés to know why he wanted to destroy their idols, for if we dishonoured them and overthrew them, that they would all perish and we along with them."[13]

Caught between the military strength of the Spanish before them and the power of Montezuma in the background, between the fear of betraying their gods and the requirement to adopt new, foreign ones, the chiefs threw up their hands and acquiesced in the smashing of their icons:

The words were hardly out of their mouths before more than fifty of us soldiers had clambered up [to the temple] and had thrown down their idols which came rolling down the steps shattered to pieces. The idols looked like fearsome dragons, as big as calves, and there were other figures half men and half great dogs of hideous appearance. When they saw their idols broken to pieces the caciques and priests who were with them wept and covered their eyes, and in the Totonac tongue they prayed [to] their gods to pardon them, saying that the matter was no longer in their hands and they were not to blame, but these Teules [godlike, powerful figures] who had overthrown them.[14]

By the time that the Spanish party had travelled about two-thirds of the way from the coast to Tenochtitlán, two months later, Cortés, his padres, and Aguilar had become adept at using intimidation and diplomacy to persuade the natives to accept the Catholic intrusion into their spiritual world. At Tlaxcala, Cortés even turned gifts from the local *caciques* into a bargaining tool. Each of five chiefs brought a daughter—attractive, well dressed, and adorned with jewellery—accompanied by a servant girl to be given to the conquistadors. To the surprise of the *caciques*, Cortés stated that he would not accept the offering until they ordered the destruction of their idols and temples and their replacement by Christian icons. When they refused his ultimatum, the Spanish leader, on the advice of his padres, compromised and accepted the young women provided that they were given Catholic baptisms and Spanish names. They were then distributed among his captains.

The giving of daughters of *caciques* to leaders of other tribes was a common practice in Mesoamerica, its purpose being, as one Tlaxcalan chief explained, "so that you may know more clearly our good will towards you and our desire to content you in everything, [and] we wish to give you our daughters, to be your wives, so that you may have children by them, for we wish to consider you as brothers as you are so good and valiant."[15] The offering of female relatives to important and powerful foreign bodies in the hope of forming alliances was not, of course, unknown in Europe, where royal households were often interrelated in complicated ways. Those transactions were conducted with more sophistication, however, and involved marriages generally recognized by all parties. In the New World, in contrast, the tribal chiefs thought that they were giving their daughters in a form of marriage, whereas the Spanish saw such offerings as merely sexual relations without obligations. Although many such native women bore children of the conquistadors, few were ever legally recognized as spouses, and they had to fight long battles to gain any form of financial support from Spain.

Aguilar talked proudly about how he had remained chaste in his years of captivity, even when his Mayan captors tempted him with a beautiful young woman. There is no way of knowing whether he remained so virtuous during the long march to Tenochtitlán and the overthrow of its Aztec rulers—he is known to have fathered at least one *mestizo* child later in life—but he would have witnessed the Spanish treatment of native women. He likely shared the attitude of the conquistadors toward the women, a mindset that suggests the worst excesses of modern barroom and dressing room male banter. Even the sober account of Díaz del Castillo approaches a smirk when he reports that one of the women given to Cortés "was named [by the Spanish] Doña Catalina, and she was very ugly; she was led by the hand and given to Cortés who received her and tried to look pleased."[16]

Such attempts at diplomacy were directed toward influential and useful *caciques* and their daughters, but little such sensitivity was shown toward less important native women. Díaz del Castillo describes how, in a town that the Spanish called Segura de la Frontera, all of the women, girls, and boys were rounded up to be branded with a symbol signifying that they had been taken in war (the men, said Díaz del Castillo, were of no use to the

Spanish). After marking them with the red-hot iron, the captains "took away and hid the best looking Indian women, and there was not a good-looking one left, and when it came to dividing them, they always allotted us the old and ugly women, and there was a great deal of grumbling about it against Cortés and those who had ordered the good-looking Indian women to be stolen and hidden." Several soldiers, complaining about the division of gold plundered from the Aztecs, concluded by saying that

> now the poor soldier who had done all the hard work and was covered with wounds could not even have a good-looking Indian woman; besides the soldiers had given the Indian women skirts and chemises, and all these women had been taken and hidden away. Moreover when the proclamation had been issued that they were to be brought and branded, it was thought that each soldier would have his women returned to him, and that they would be appraised according to the value of each in pesos.... When Cortés saw this, he said with smooth words (for that was his usual oath) that from that time forward he would not act in that way, but that good or bad, all the Indian women should be put up for auction, and that the good-looking ones should be sold for so much, those that were not good looking for a lower price, so that there should be no cause of quarrel with him.[17]

By the time that Cortés was seizing control of the territory surrounding Tenochtitlán, the capture of attractive native women was becoming an obsession among his men. Writing about the events some decades later, Díaz del Castillo suggests that this goal outweighed all others. Having routed the enemy in one battle, he reported, the Spanish soldiers did not pursue the retreating warriors because "they were chiefly occupied in looking out for pretty Indian women or seeking for plunder.... Sandoval and all his army returned to Texcoco with much spoil, especially of good-looking women."[18] A few pages later Díaz del Castillo describes entering a town called Tepostlán, where "we found some very good-looking Indian women and much spoil,"[19] and in a neighbouring community "we took great spoil both of large bales of cloth as well as good-looking women."[20]

The interactions of Spanish invaders and indigenous women, during the march to Tenochtitlán, the conquest of the Aztecs, and the subsequent settlement period, had a profound influence on the history of Mexico. According to R. C. Padden,

> the primary conquest of Mexico was really more biological than military. However strenuous the fighting was at times, love-making was just as intense, certainly more frequent, and of infinitely greater consequence. Although it cannot be statistically proved or disproved, I would guess that the Spaniards commonly left more pregnancies in their camps than they did casualties on the field of battle. Biologically speaking, it was neither microbe nor sword nor mailed fist that conquered Mexico. It was the *membrum febrilis* [fevered male sex organ].[21]

Even if Padden has exaggerated the consequence of Spanish sexual dominance of native women—in effect their rape—it has had a deep meaning in a country comprising 60 per cent mestizos. Symbolically, if not factually, the fusion of Mexico's two principal races, Spanish and native, was created by the violence of the conquerors or the willing collusion of the conquered. And this symbolism has become represented by one of the most famous women in Mexican history, a native who fell into the hands of Cortés and his party and became not only an essential element of his defeat of the Aztecs but also his lover. Called Malinche or Malintzin by her own people and Marina by the Spanish, she came to embody the native woman's role as either rape victim or traitor:

Perhaps no native American woman has been as implicated in this particular discourse as the much maligned "La Malinche," Cortés's famous interpreter and lover. From nationalist Mexican rhetoric to twentieth-century Chicana feminist works, La Malinche, or Doña Marina, has consistently been dragged through the mud of rape, sexual promiscuity, treachery, treason, and dupery. In popular Mexican history she and Cortés are figured as the parents of the first mestizo and hence the mother and father of today's Mexico—a highly conflicted national heritage.[22]

Malinche joined the Cortés party after it had skirted the Yucatán Peninsula, at Tabasco, where the local *caciques* gave her and nineteen other native women to the Spanish. Cortés, recalled Díaz del Castillo, "received this present with pleasure and went aside with all the Caciques, and with Aguilar, the interpreter, to hold converse." The next day one of the company's padres, Fray Bartolomé de Olmedo,

> with Aguilar as interpreter, preached many good things about our holy faith to the twenty Indian women who had been given us, and immediately afterwards they were baptized. One Indian lady...who was given us here was christened Doña Marina, and she was truly a great chieftainess and the daughter of great Caciques and the mistress of vassals, and this her appearance clearly showed.[23]

Like most of early Mexican history, the story of Malinche has been written, rewritten, revised, speculated about, interpreted, and reinterpreted so that, in Townsend's words, "certainty is elusive."[24] As her own meticulously researched and carefully developed narrative shows, however, some things can be said with confidence about Malinche. Born in the early years of the sixteenth century in Coatzacoalcos, a state in central Mexico bordering the

Gulf of Mexico, she belonged to the Nahua, a tribe on the outer reaches of the large grouping now called Aztec. Her birth name is unknown, though some historians have suggested that she was called Malinalli Tenepal; it is much more likely that she was called Malintzin, which to Spanish ears sounded like Malinche. Díaz del Castillo might have exaggerated her status by calling her the daughter of "great Caciques," but she seems to have been born into an affluent and fairly eminent family.

This life of privilege and comfort ended sometime between the ages of eight and twelve when Malinche was taken by slave traders from her village, downriver to the Gulf of Mexico, and then about 150 miles east along the coast. According to Díaz del Castillo, her father had died, and her mother remarried another chief and gave birth to a son. Seemingly to get rid of Malinche and thus smooth the way for the son to become the *cacique*, her mother found it convenient to sell her to passing slave traders. As Townsend points out, there are reasons to doubt some of the details of this narrative, but unquestionably the young girl was betrayed into slavery by some of her own people. She was taken to a port called Xicallanco, on the huge Laguna de Términos, and sold to some Chontal Maya, who took her back westward on the coast to Tabasco. Within a few years of living there, she had learned to speak both Chontal Maya and the considerably different Yucatec Maya; such linguistic skill, together with her native Nahuatl, was rare and would make her extraordinarily valuable to Cortés.

Malinche fell into the hands of the Spanish party when, following defeat in a fierce battle, the Chontal Mayan *caciques* presented Cortés with the twenty female slaves, not as potential wives but as sexual objects. Each of the women was passed on to one of the captains, and Malinche, newly christened Doña Marina, was awarded to Alonso Hernández Puertocarrero. She was, said Díaz del Castillo, "good looking and intelligent and without embarrassment."[25]

Like all such native female slaves given to the Spanish, Malinche was destined to serve as a sex object until Puertocarrero tired of her and passed her on to one of the lower-ranking soldiers. Indeed, several weeks later in Cempoala, her position became even more tenuous when Cortés again provided his favourite captain with the gift of a comely daughter of a prominent *cacique*. By then, however, Malinche had revealed skills far more important to Cortés than those of the bedchamber: she could speak Nahuatl, the language of the people of the Mexican mainland, the Aztecs into whose territory the Spanish commander intended to penetrate deeply.

When Cortés first encountered representatives of Montezuma, at a Gulf of Mexico town that Grijalva had called San Juan de Ulúa, he was "vexed…exceedingly" by discovering that Aguilar was unable to communicate with them. He knew Yucatec Maya, but the Mayan family of languages was entirely unrelated to Classical Nahuatl, the language of the Aztec Empire. The expedition had gone beyond the Yucatecans, passed through the Chontal Mayan territory, and now needed to deal with natives who spoke Nahuatl. By good fortune, members of the Cortés party spotted Malinche talking easily and knowledgeably with some of the Nahua men, and, according to López de Gómara, "Cortés took her aside with Aguilar and promised her more than her liberty if she would establish friendship between him and the men of her country, and he told her that he would like to have her for his interpreter and secretary."[26] Thus was created a complicated but workable system of translation in which the Aztecs spoke with Malinche, who then passed on the message to Aguilar in Yucatec Maya, and he was able to deliver it in Spanish to Cortés. From that point until the fall of Tenochtitlán, Malinche and Aguilar formed one of history's most famous interpreting partnerships, and they were at the side of Cortés at every meeting with *caciques* and other native leaders. They were essential to his conversations and negotiations with Montezuma.

Finding Aguilar in Yucatán had been a stroke of luck for Cortés, and the expedition would likely have foundered without his knowledge of the Mayan tongue. Ultimately, however, Malinche became the more useful and influential interpreter, and there is little doubt that the Spanish could not have defeated Montezuma's Aztecs—at least as quickly as they did—without her. She had an aristocratic bearing that impressed both the Spanish—who took the unusual step of calling her Doña Marina—and the *caciques*—who took the equally unusual step of addressing Cortés by a variation of her name, Malinche, because he was so often by her side.

Since she was a Nahua, there was always the danger that, like Melchorejo, her sympathies would lie with the enemy and that ultimately she would betray the Spanish. However, her own betrayal by the Nahua when she was sold into slavery, and her loathing of the dominance of Montezuma's Aztecs over the region, seem to have made Malinche totally loyal to the Cortés party. Aguilar undoubtedly had long conversations with her in which he told her about Spain—its history, monarchy, social structure, and religion—and she wholeheartedly adopted its values. As time went by, she proved to be as trustworthy as Aguilar, and, after the fall of Tenochtitlán, when she had become fluent in Spanish, she rendered him unnecessary. Her unqualified adoption of the values of Mexico's conquerors, however, ultimately made her a complicated and ambiguous figure for generations far into the future.

Serving as a loyal and trusted interpreter for the Spanish would have been enough for Malinche to be considered a traitor by many Mexicans, but she became a much more controversial figure when Cortés also took her as a mistress. In July 1519, he sent Puertocarrero and Francisco de Montejo to Spain to convey news of his expedition, take petitions for support, and deliver considerable treasure to the king. Puertocarrero did not return to Mexico for several years, and shortly after his departure for Spain Malinche shrewdly attached herself to Cortés or was simply appropriated by him. In any case, she lived with Cortés in Coyoacán, near Tenochtitlán, and bore him a son, called Martín, in 1522.

While Malinche was pregnant, Catalina Suárez, whom Cortés had married in Cuba, arrived and took up residence as his wife until her mysterious death during the night of All Saints' Day.

In 1524, Malinche was either passed on to one of the captains, Juan Jaramillo, or seized the opportunity to gain a security that she would never have with Cortés. Whatever the reason, she married Jaramillo, reportedly drunk at the time of the ceremony, and bore him a daughter, María. Malinche served as an interpreter for Cortés on his march through what is now Honduras in a fruitless search for a strait connecting the Atlantic and Pacific. She died, likely from one of the European diseases that ravaged the people of the New World, early in 1529, though some historians place her death two decades later.

In five extensive letters from Cortés to the Spanish monarch about his conquest of Mexico, Malinche is mentioned only twice, once briefly by name and once as "my interpreter, who is an Indian woman from Puntunchan."[27] She was not mentioned in his will, but their son, Martín, was given 1,000 gold ducats a year for life. Although Cortés was very fond of him, took him to Spain, and had him legitimized by Pope Clement VII in 1529, it was a legitimately born half-brother, also called Martín, who inherited the title of Marquis of the Valley of Oaxaca and control of their father's estate. In Mexico in 1565, the two Martíns, along with another half-brother, were accused of plotting a rebellion against Spain, and Malinche's son was savagely tortured before being released for lack of evidence. He returned to Spain, joined the military, and died in battle a few years later helping the Spanish put down a Muslim rebellion in Granada. In López de Gómara's biography of Cortés, Martín is mentioned once, briefly identified as a son "whom [Cortés] had by an Indian woman."[28]

María, born only a short time before her mother's death, had a long and exhausting struggle to be recognized as a legitimate heir to Jaramillo's estate, part of which had been a wedding gift from Cortés to Malinche. Jaramillo had quickly remarried—to an upper-class young Spanish woman named Doña Beatriz de Andrade—and become wealthy, and on his death around 1550 María learned that she would inherit only a third of her father's holdings. When she contested the will, her stepmother argued that "the Indian woman...Marina...had been rewarded more than she deserved in marrying...Jaramillo, for he lost much honor in the marriage."[29] The case dragged on in the Spanish courts for more than two decades, during which Doña Beatriz alleged that Malinche had never been an important interpreter and perhaps had even been a traitor. When the court finally ruled in 1573 that María's claim was unproven, María had been dead for ten years.

Malinche's son by Cortés and daughter by Jaramillo clearly suffered from having "that Indian woman" as their mother, being denied the titles and the legacy that they would have received as legitimately born Spaniards. But even many of the important Spanish participants in the Cortés expedition seem to have fallen into the pattern common to so many of Spain's New World explorers: discontent with and lengthy litigation over their rewards and jealous arguments about the parts that they had played in the conquest of Mexico. Cortés himself ended his life as a disillusioned and embittered old man. He was not, like Balboa, beheaded for treason or murdered like Pizarro or executed like Pizarro's brother Gonzalo. He was not, like Columbus, disgraced as a colonial administrator, arrested, and taken in chains to Spain. But like the great navigator of the Ocean Sea, he did live to see the bureaucrats in Seville appoint lesser men to govern the lands that his daring and skill had acquired for his monarch, and he spent many of his days in the vain hope that he could still discover new realms. He died in 1547 before he could return to Mexico, where he would become so despised by indigenous people that his remains, buried there as he had wished, ultimately had to be interred in secret.

A trusted former aide of Cortés who turned against him in the years following the defeat of the Aztecs was Aguilar, whom Cortés had rescued from Mayan captivity. Aguilar had worked well with Malinche throughout the march to Tenochtitlán and the defeat of Montezuma, indeed was rumoured to have wanted her for himself; but, as she became more fluent in Spanish and more intimate with

Cortés, Aguilar became less important. He seems to have become resentful of her influence with his commander, and in 1529 he launched two lawsuits against Cortés. One of his charges was that there was a secret door to the conquistador's house in Coyoacán by which undisclosed tribute could be hidden so as to avoid paying the royal fifth to the Spanish crown. Cortés responded by claiming that any deliveries to that entrance were of goods such as incense, tobacco, and fruit for Malinche's personal use.

Despite his lawsuits, Aguilar had been treated generously, though not by Cortés, in the division of the spoils of conquest. In 1526, when Cortés was back in Spain, the triumvirate ruling Mexico in his absence appointed Aguilar *encomendero* of both Molango and Malila and of Sochicoatlán, two substantial tracts of land northeast of the capital. The *encomienda*, created in the early sixteenth century, was a form of slave holding in which a person, usually as a reward for services to the crown, was given land and its natives, who were to provide labour and tribute. In return, the *encomendero* was entrusted to take care of the natives, defend them against others, and educate them in the Christian faith; but these obligations were often ignored and the natives abused.

Aguilar was particularly favoured by being given *encomiendas* near Mexico City; Díaz del Castillo, in contrast, was given land in Guatemala and eventually died poor. In seven years, Aguilar had gone from Mayan slave to semi-feudal lord, a remarkable rise for someone plucked from the Yucatán jungle, an unknown quantity to Cortés, and placed among a force of 500 or so conquistadors and soldiers already assembled. The one thing that he is known to have taken from the Maya, an ability to speak their language, elevated him from castaway to major participant in the conquest of Mexico. He began as Cortés's translator, a liaison between invader and invaded, and he ended as a quasi-conquistador, as eager to subjugate the defeated peoples as any empire builder.

Aguilar lived in Mexico City in comfort, supported by the labour of the natives and the income from his *encomienda*, but he did not enjoy this life for long. He died in his forties in 1531, reportedly suffering from buboes, a symptom, among other things, of syphilis and gonorrhea. He had never married, so his *encomienda* reverted to the crown. The chastity that he had claimed to have maintained in the face of the temptation during his Mayan captivity did not survive his years as interpreter and *encomendero*. Aguilar developed a relationship with a Topoyanco native woman, christened Elvira Toznenetzin, and had two daughters, one of whom was referred to in a court document dated "Mexico, 1554." This material was filed "in support of a petition for payment for military services under Cortés, by one Cristóbal Doria, of Oaxaca, the husband by a 'legitimate church marriage' with Luisa, the natural daughter of Gerónimo de Aguilar, had by him 'an unmarried bachelor, and free' by an unnamed Tarascan woman."[30]

Aguilar thus remains an enigmatic and complicated figure, a pliable character for authors who have attempted to define him in fiction. As a figure in early Mexican history, he is especially interesting when considered alongside his fellow castaway Guerrero. Despite the violence of the shipwreck and the dislocation of his captivity, he maintained his Catholic faith, his Eurocentrism, and his belief in Spanish hegemony. He thrived on his return to his countrymen and became a translator, a go-between, a facilitator of conquest, a figure situated between the Spanish invaders and the defeated indigenous peoples. And for a few years he reaped the rewards of the conqueror.

Guerrero's translation, on the other hand, was not of the words— devious, unstable, and ephemeral—of others but of himself. The sailor from Palos had reinvented himself as a Mayan warrior, and he stood unequivocally and proudly among his adopted people. Was he as content in his village at Chactemal as Aguilar was ruling his *encomienda* near Mexico City? We will never know. But one thing is certain: Guerrero would have to defend his life there as vigorously as he had ever defended anything.

CHAPTER SEVEN

"Gonzalo, My Brother and Special Friend":
GUERRERO THE WARRIOR AND THE BATTLE FOR YUCATÁN

And what of the legend of Gonzalo the warrior? Guerrero had declined the invitation from Cortés to join his forces, and by doing so he missed the opportunity to share in the glory of the conquest of Tenochtitlán. It might have been his name, rather than that of Jerónimo de Aguilar, that appeared so frequently in Bernal Díaz del Castillo's history and his partnership with Malinche that helped to bring down Montezuma and the Aztec Empire. He might then have lived well into old age as an affluent and powerful landowner on the spoils of conquest. Or he might have returned to Yucatán to use his knowledge and understanding of the Maya to secure that peninsula for Spain, a conquest that ultimately took several more decades and cost hundreds of Spanish lives. Such possibilities would have been beyond even the wildest dreams of the young man who left Palos years before to seek his fortune in the New World. Instead, Gonzalo chose to remain with his Mayan wife and mixed-race children, living among a people and culture unlike anything that he had known in his early life.

Today, in the Governor's Palace in the central plaza of Mérida, there is a set of twenty-six remarkable paintings on public display. These huge murals, commissioned from the Yucatán painter Fernando Castro Pacheco in the early 1970s, provide a striking history of the Yucatán Peninsula. With a remarkable candour, a civic willingness to address the evils of the colonial past with an openness rarely seen in the rest of North America, the paintings tell the history of the region, from the creation myth of the Maya to the mid-nineteenth-century Caste War. Among the graphic representations of enslaved natives, tortured native rebels, greedy landlords, bloodstained conquistadors, and unbending clergymen is a striking portrait of Guerrero, his Mayan wife, and one of their children.

The picture is not an accurate rendering of Gonzalo as he would have appeared after years of living among the Maya: there are no nose rings, ear plugs, or tattoos; his hair is not cut and shaped in the Mayan style; he is wearing mid-thigh-length trousers rather than the native loincloth; and the upper half of his body is as white as—indeed probably whiter than—the day he left Spain. Clearly more symbolic than realistic, the painting represents the creation of the Mexican *mestizo*, not through brutal conquest but through peaceful accommodation and compromise. Gonzalo's body is that of a sturdy, powerful labourer, and on his face is both an expression of resolute determination and a sadness, or at least an uncertainty, in the eyes. His large hand protectively encloses that of Zazil Há, who stands as if guarded by his frame, beside and a bit behind him; in sharp contrast to his whiteness, she is painted in dark copper tones. On Gonzalo's other arm sits a naked baby with the dark almond eyes of his mother and the same down-turned mouth, but the child is bathed in a colour halfway between those in which Gonzalo and Zazil Há are portrayed. Lying abandoned on the ground under one of Gonzalo's feet, and barely noticeable to a viewer, is his Spanish sword.

The Pacheco painting is a counterweight to the statues of Guerrero depicting him as an armed warrior; this is a man who simply wants to live a quiet pastoral life with his Mayan family. Whether Guerrero was ever able to enjoy such a peaceful existence, however, is unlikely. He had risen, after all, to the rank of *nacom*, or captain, among the Chactemal Maya because of his military leadership in battles with quarrelsome opposing tribes. Then, too, he seems to have served the Maya well as an adviser about the bearded, strangely clad, and terrifyingly armed intruders who began to appear along the shores of Yucatán. According to some Spanish chroniclers, he might even have led the native forces in combat against the earliest invaders.

In the first battle between the Spanish and the Maya in Yucatán, the ambush of the expedition led by Francisco Hernández de Córdoba at Cape Catoche in 1517, the attack seems to have been driven by a knowledge of what the intruders were capable of doing, the brutality of their incursions into other parts of the Caribbean. Inga Clendinnen points out that, though stories of Spanish conduct might have drifted onto the Yucatán Peninsula from the occasional trading canoe, the Maya certainly had knowledge of it from the survivors of the 1512 shipwreck.[1] From what is known about each man, that information is much more likely to have come from Guerrero than from Aguilar.

Hernández de Córdoba's second battle with Mayan warriors, a humiliating rout of the Spanish a month later on the west coast of the Yucatán Peninsula at Champotón, also suggests that the natives had been forewarned about the intruders. Once again the Maya were well prepared and aware of the origins of the invaders: their leaders asked if the Spanish had come from the direction of the sunrise, and they repeated the words that the Spanish had first heard at Campeche: "*Castilan, Castilan.*"

Although there is no evidence to confirm the claims of some historians that Guerrero fought with the Maya at Champotón, he might have been there either as an adviser or as a captain. The territory between Chactemal and Campeche is the narrowest stretch of land on the Yucatán Peninsula, and a *sacbe*, one of the raised and paved Mayan roads, ran between the two communities. Communication would have been good, and overland travel would have been easier than in many other parts of the peninsula. With his knowledge of the strange new intruders, Guerrero would have been a valuable resource for the Maya, and Nachan Ka'an might well have sent him with a party of warriors to assist the natives at Champotón.

When the expedition led by Juan de Grijalva reached Campeche, Champotón, and Tabasco a year later, the natives did not offer the same armed resistance, seeming to prefer a different strategy, one that indigenous peoples elsewhere had learned to use with the Spanish. Offering some gold ornaments to Grijalva's party, the natives pointed westward and said "*Colua, Colua, Méjico, Méjico.*" The Hernández de Córdoba party had gone ashore far more interested in finding fresh water, of which they had desperate need, than gold or silver, yet the natives whom Grijalva faced seemed to know of the Spanish obsession with riches, what Hernán Cortés later told the Aztecs was "a disease of the heart which can be cured only with gold."[2] Someone who would have understood that malady well was Guerrero.

When Cortés mounted his expedition in 1519, he was driven by the dramatic news that Grijalva had brought back to Cuba, stories of the gold that he had found and the promise of much more of it in the lands beyond Campeche and Champotón. As a result, he largely ignored Yucatán and pushed into the interior of Mexico to Tenochtitlán, where his conquest of the Aztecs and his plundering of their treasure drew the attention of the Spanish away from Yucatán, which had yielded little gold and silver. Cortés himself led an expedition into Guatemala and Honduras in 1524, in part to find a strait connecting the Atlantic and Pacific Oceans and in part in response to rumours of gold in such abundance that fishermen weighted their nets with it. Thus, if Guerrero was ever able to enjoy a simple, relatively peaceful, and pastoral life among the

Maya portrayed by Pacheco, then it was during the eight years following the Cortés invasion of mainland Mexico. During that time, Spanish ships were seen offshore as they ferried goods and settlers to Mexico and treasure back to Spain, but there was no incursion into Yucatán beyond the occasional foray in search of water.

Word of the death of Montezuma, the fall of Tenochtitlán, and the brutal treatment of its people spread quickly throughout the region, and their impacts—for example the shrivelling of the lucrative trade between Guerrero's Chactemal tribe and the Aztec communities toward the mainland of Mexico—were felt in Yucatán. The Cortés trek down into Honduras, moreover, would have reminded Gonzalo that the Spanish appetite for conquest was insatiable. But it was not until 1527 that such hunger brought his former countrymen back to Yucatán determined to turn it into another Spanish colony. In December 1526, a member of the Grijalva expedition and one of the original Cortés captains, Francisco de Montejo, was granted a *capitulación* or "charter" by the Spanish crown to conquer and colonize the Yucatán Peninsula. He was named *adelantado*, or "governor," of Yucatán, a title given to him and his successors in perpetuity. Indeed, it would take more than one generation of Montejos to subdue the Maya of the peninsula in a struggle that would drag on for many more years than the conquests of the Aztecs and Incas, and take more Spanish lives than the other two campaigns combined.

Montejo had been sent back to Spain in July 1519 to work on behalf of Cortés at the Spanish court, so he missed the great march into Mexico and the capturing of Tenochtitlán. During his five months with the Spanish force along the coast of Yucatán, however, he talked frequently with Aguilar and learned a great deal about the Maya, the land, the climate, and the environment. Back in Spain, he came to think that what he thought was the island of Yucatán—the huge expanse of water at the Laguna de Términos had persuaded him that it was a body of land separate from the mainland—had its own riches and was suitable for colonizing.

Subduing the Maya and seizing control of Yucatán presented formidable challenges. Unlike the Aztecs in Mexico and the Inca in Peru, the Maya were not ruled by an emperor situated in a central capital city. Centuries earlier, power had been centralized in Uxmal and Chichén Itzá, but the last centre to exercise control over a confederation of Yucatán tribes was Mayapán (meaning "Banner of the Maya"), a city located in the north-central part of the peninsula. About 1441, however, political quarrelling among its leaders led to a rebellion in which the ruling family was killed; the city was sacked, burned, and abandoned; and Yucatán became a region of warring city-states. There was thus no head that Montejo could cut off to disable the body; he had to overpower various arms and limbs all over the peninsula. The defeat of one tribe did little to diminish the resistance of the others.

Adding to Montejo's difficulty were the formidable fighting abilities of the Maya, no matter what part of Yucatán they were defending. A Mayan warrior carried fearsome weapons: long spears with heads of sharpened stone or copper, javelins and darts made of wood with fire-hardened points, bows and stone-tipped arrows, slings and stones. Particularly lethal were *macanas* or *maquahuitls*, "two-handed wooden swords" three to four feet long and three inches wide. Grooves running along both edges contained jagged pieces of flint or obsidian, and these shards, like the heads of the spears and arrows, splintered on striking an enemy. This created particularly savage and lethal wounds, with death often coming after weeks of agony.

An attack by Mayan warriors in full battle mode was a frightening spectacle. From their necks to their knees, they wore material made from strongly twisted cord and quilted cotton, an armour so effective that arrows could not penetrate it, and they carried sturdy shields. Their faces were painted black and white, or red and white, and their bodies were painted black or red. They wore their hair free-flowing or tied so as to make them fierce looking, and they often sported large and colourful feathered crests on their heads.

As they swarmed toward the Spanish, they let out piercing, high-pitched whistles, a sound accompanied by the beat of war drums and the bugling of conch shell horns. The effect on the Spanish, as Díaz del Castillo described it, was intimidating:

> How they began to charge on us! What hail of stones sped from their slings! As for their bowmen, the javelins lay like corn on the threshing floor; all of them barbed and fire-hardened, which would pierce any amour and would reach the vitals where there is no protection; the men with swords and shields and other arms larger than swords, such as broadswords, and lances, how they pressed on us and with what valour and what mighty shouts and yells they charged upon us![3]

The natives, he said, "cast stones from their slings in such numbers that they fell like hail."[4]

The Mayan warriors had the advantage of fighting on familiar terrain, a landscape unfamiliar to European soldiers. It was particularly difficult for the Spanish to manoeuvre on: uniformly flat with very few landmarks—lakes, rivers, or heights of land—by which a fighting force could orient itself. The Maya knew the locations of the *cenotes*, the "sinkholes" that were the only sources of fresh water, and they were familiar with the network of narrow paths that criss-crossed Yucatán with the intricacy of a spider web. The paths, moreover, were much more suited to the swift movement of lightly clad Mayan warriors than the lumbering progress of Spanish fighting men. "Paths," says Clendinnen,

> comfortably wide for the smooth-trotting Maya, body bowed, possessions slung neatly in a carrying net along the back, were miserably narrow for the European foot soldier, lugging his clumsy weapons and, where natives could not be pressed into service, whatever food he had been able to

gather or loot. For the horseman, hacking away at over-hanging branches, his mount plunging and slithering, it was frustrating, constant, unproductive exertion.[5]

Added to the torment of battling unyielding vegetation were clouds of mosquitoes and legions of large stinging black ants and *garrapatas*, "small burrowing ticks" that left inflamed and easily infected abscesses. But the jungle undergrowth held greater dangers. A common Mayan tactic was to construct a palisade at an especially narrow point of a path, interweaving vines and leaves through it and the surrounding dense bush. Silent and unseen behind this seemingly impenetrable vegetation, the natives ambushed the Spanish with streams of arrows, darts, lances, and stones.

And the Maya had Guerrero.

The Spanish, however, had centuries of technology shaping their combat. They had metal lances, shields, swords, and armour, though by the time of Montejo's expedition they had wisely abandoned the heavy steel armour for the lighter and more comfortable native quilted cotton suit. Their horses were protected by their own quilted armour, but they were only a little less frightening to the natives than they had been when Cortés first brought them to Yucatán. The Spanish crossbows were effective weapons, but the cannons and flintlock harquebuses not only inflicted lethal wounds on the natives but also terrorized them with their explosions.

The Spanish also had, at least in the early conflicts with the Maya, a superior combat strategy. For centuries, the Maya had focused not on killing their enemies in battle but on capturing them for use as slaves or sacrifices; this they did by a direct, frontal assault, charging into their foes with clubs and spears. The Spanish, however, followed European tradition in wanting to kill their adversaries as many and as quickly as possible, and they cut a wide swath in the native forces with their superior weaponry. Díaz del Castillo frequently describes such confrontations in the Hernández de Córdoba and Grijalva forays and in the early stages of the Cortés expedition, when the natives rushed the Spaniards like "mad dogs" and were cut down by cannon, muskets, and crossbows.[6] As time went by and the Maya became more familiar with the Spanish, they abandoned the direct assault in favour of ambushes, flanking manoeuvres, and trickery. Although it cannot be proven, some chroniclers were convinced that the impetus for this change of strategy came from Guerrero. "When a little more than a year ago," Díaz del Castillo reported Aguilar as saying, "a captain and three vessels arrived at Cape Catoche, it was at the suggestion of Guerrero that the natives attacked them, and he was there himself in the company of the cacique of the large town."[7]

Because of his experience with the Grijalva and Cortés expeditions, Montejo knew that he would have to be well prepared and well armed to subdue the Maya. With funds provided by the sale of inherited property in Salamanca and through a shrewd marriage to a wealthy widow of Seville, he was able to mount an impressive and well-provisioned armada of four ships and 400 men, and he appointed Alonso Dávila as his second in command. Dávila, like his leader, had served on the Grijalva expedition, and he had distinguished himself as a courageous, shrewd, daring, and capable captain under Cortés. Montejo had a chief pilot familiar with the Yucatán coastline, fifty cavalrymen, a good stock of cannon and other arms, and essential foods to last for a year. When he sailed out of the southern port of San Lúcar de Barrameda for the New World in June 1527, he called his flotilla "the best that has come out from Castile."[8]

After taking on more supplies in Hispaniola, the armada sailed to Cozumel and then to the small village of Xelha on the mainland. After ordering the *Requerimiento* to be read out in a lively ceremony that ended with the raising of the royal standard and the cry of "*España, España, España, viva!*" Montejo chose that site for the first Spanish settlement in Yucatán. He named it Salamanca de Xelha, the first of four towns that he would name after his place of birth, none of which ultimately survived. His forces faced severe hardships almost immediately, finding that the foods were insufficient, and the wet, hot climate and lack of drinkable fresh water led to the settlement being ravaged by a particularly virulent disease. Within two months, fifty men were dead. The local natives were uncooperative and adopted a strategy of passive resistance, melting into the jungle rather than defying the Spanish or engaging in actual battle.

To head off a possible mutiny by men wanting to abandon the excursion, Montejo imitated his former commander, Cortés, and sank his ships. He then led a march northward up the coast to Cabo Catoche, the site on the northeast point of Yucatán first seen by the Hernández de Córdoba expedition a decade earlier. On returning to Salamanca de Xelha several months later, he found only a third of his forces still alive, leaving him with fewer than 100 men. On the positive side, the party was strengthened by the arrival of a supply ship from Hispaniola, so Montejo decided to explore the southeastern coast of Yucatán in the hope of finding a more favourable location for a colony. The southern region had better soil, more rain, and lusher vegetation than the northern region; the great Bahía de Chetumal offered the possibility of a much better harbour; and the more numerous lakes and rivers promised better water and easier travel. But it also had Guerrero.

Montejo knew a good deal about Guerrero from his conversations with Aguilar, but he does not seem to have known that he was living among the Chactemal Maya until he began questioning three or four natives captured on a night raid. When he learned of the Spaniard-turned-Maya's proximity to him, Montejo saw an opportunity to fill a serious deficiency in his company. Although he had witnessed the significant contribution that Aguilar's skill as an interpreter had made to the success of Cortés in dealing with the Yucatán Maya, he had not found an interpreter for his own journey of conquest. Having lived among the Maya for a much longer period than Aguilar, and more intimately aware of their culture and behaviour, Guerrero would be an invaluable aid.

That is, if he could be persuaded to return to his own people and to the Christian faith.

According to Gonzalo Fernández de Oviedo, Montejo gave one of the captured natives the following message to be taken to Guerrero:

Gonzalo, my brother and special friend, I count it my good fortune that I arrived and have learned of you through the bearer of this letter, [through which] I can remind you that you are a Christian, bought by the blood of Jesus Christ, our Redeemer, to whom I give, and you should give, infinite thanks. You have a great opportunity to serve God and the Emperor, Our Lord, in the pacification and baptism of these people, and more than this, [an opportunity] to leave your sins behind you, with the Grace of God, and to honor and benefit yourself. I shall be your very good friend in this, and you will be treated very well.

And thus I beseech you not to let the devil influence you not to do what I say, so that he will not possess himself of you forever.

On behalf of His Majesty I promise you to do very well for you and fully to comply with that which I have said. On my part, as a noble gentleman, I give you my word and pledge my faith to make any promises to you good without any reservations whatsoever, favoring and honoring you and making you one of my principal men and one of my most select and loved groups in these parts.

Consequently [I beseech] you to come to this ship, or to the coast, without delay, to do what I have said and to help me carry out, through giving me your counsel and opinions, that which seems most expedient.[9]

Montejo's appeal, at least in Fernández de Oviedo's version, was more carefully crafted than that of Cortés nine years earlier, no doubt informed by what Montejo had learned of Guerrero from his conversations with Aguilar. He counted on reawakening Guerrero's Catholicism and suggesting that Guerrero could best serve the natives among whom he lived by bringing them to the Christian faith. In case he could be moved by more practical concerns, Montejo promised Guerrero power as one of his "principal men," with his tribe becoming one of the "most select and loved" communities in the region. Had Guerrero accepted the offer from Cortés years earlier, he would have been part of the great conquest of the Aztecs and, like Aguilar, become a prosperous *encomendero*, but of course he could not have known what lay ahead for the Spanish in Mexico. Montejo's overture, on the other hand, was specific and promised an immediate return to his own race, among whom he would be given a position of authority.

Montejo's entreaty was never likely to succeed, no matter how shrewdly tailored: his man had lived among the Maya for sixteen years and was then irretrievably embedded in the culture, the indigenous faith, and his family and community. His children, young when Aguilar had come to him with the letter from Cortés, were then approaching adolescence, and Guerrero would have known how they would fare as newly christened, newly named young natives in a Spanish colony. His Mayan wife was unlikely to be treated any better, and certainly not with the respect in which she was held in Chactemal. And, if Guerrero was barely distinguishable from the natives after seven years of living among them, how much more complete was his transformation after sixteen years? Having rejected the offer from Cortés following a limited separation from his Spanish countrymen, he would be highly unlikely to accept the offer from Montejo after more than twice that time in the jungle.

Guerrero did not waste much time in responding to Montejo, the next day scribbling an ironic reply in charcoal on the back of the *adelantado*'s letter: "Señor, I kiss your Grace's hands. As I am a slave I have no freedom [to accept your offer], even though I am married and have a wife and children, I remember God. You, my Lord and the Spanish will find in me a very good friend."[10]

The phrasing of this note, said to be from a sixteenth-century sailor who had not spoken Spanish for a dozen years, likely owes more to Fernández de Oviedo than to Guerrero; however it was worded, the rejection must have stirred various emotions in Montejo. He might have been surprised that Guerrero did not share his certainty of the rightness of the Spanish chivalric ethos of conquest of foreign lands and destruction of pagan religions. He almost certainly would have felt indignation that his "brother and special friend" had rejected his offer in such a flippant fashion. In recounting the episode, Fernández de Oviedo speaks for the Spanish of the time in his contempt for the apostate sailor:

This Gonzalo, mariner, who was of the Condado de Niebla,…was already converted into an Indian and was married to an Indian woman. He had his ears mutilated and his tongue cut in sacrificial fashion, and had his body painted like a native.…This evil person, as he must have been from his origins, [born and] brought up among low and vile people, and one who was not well taught nor properly instructed in the elements of our Holy Catholic Faith, or who was by chance [which must be suspected]…of low race and suspect of not being of the Christian religion, took the letter Montejo sent to him by this Indian and read it.[11]

When Cortés responded to Guerrero's rejection of his offer by saying that "it will never do to leave him here," he was making a general observation. It was a comment about a fellow Spaniard left among the savages, though Aguilar had claimed that his fellow castaway had been behind the Mayan attacks on Hernández de Córdoba and Grijalva. Cortés did not know much about Yucatán and had no intention of occupying it, so any Guerrero-led native resistance would be the problem of some subsequent conquistador. For Montejo, however, the stakes were much higher: he had been given a licence to colonize the peninsula, and a hostile Guerrero would always stand in the way of a complete conquest and an acquiescent native population. He was a captain in one of the largest, most powerful tribes in the region, one centred in the most difficult and desirable terrains in Yucatán, and his knowledge of Spanish military strategy could make the Maya formidable enemies.

It did not take long for Montejo to discover that Guerrero was indeed a wily opponent. The *adelantado* had sailed from Salamanca de Xelha with a small party while Dávila had been sent overland with the greater number of soldiers to meet his commander at Chactemal. Dávila's assignment was formidable since, in addition to the absence of clearly defined roads and paths and the presence of various tormenting insects in the heat and humidity of the jungle, his route was marked by several large bays, the Bahía de Ascensión and the Bahía de Espíritu Santo, which drove Dávila much farther inland than he wished to go. As he got closer to Chactemal, he was kept well away from the coast by the many impenetrable swamps and lagoons, and he seems to have been led even farther off course by false information given to him by local natives. He finally managed to reach a point about 120 kilometres from Chactemal, but he had no knowledge of the whereabouts of Montejo or whether he had even survived. Terrain and native strategies successfully kept the Spanish parties apart and ignorant of the location of each other.

Respected historian of Yucatán Robert S. Chamberlain suggests that this strategy of division and misinformation was directed by Guerrero:

With his military talent and prestige among the Indians, it is possible that he may have been important in organizing Maya resistance throughout the peninsula and in teaching the natives new methods of warfare which were best calculated to be effective against his former countrymen. Certainly he must have had a hand in the expulsion of Dávila from the southern provinces. Some Spaniards openly attributed their military reverses to Guerrero's genius.[12]

There is no way of knowing how much of the Mayan resistance to the Montejo incursion was engineered by Guerrero. All of the chroniclers believe that he was then still a prominent captain in the Chactemal tribe, and as such he would undoubtedly have been an important counsel to Nachan Ka'an. Moreover, the native campaign against Montejo in southern Yucatán was more coordinated, more cunning, and more aware of Spanish strategies and psychology than anything faced by earlier conquistadors. Dávila and Montejo did not merely confront hordes of natives charging at them from the jungle, but also were up against a knowledgeable and clever strategist who would defeat them by deception.

The first act of trickery was to have the natives around the Dávila encampment spread the word that the Montejo party had perished. Given the hazards of navigating the Caribbean, the ruggedness of much of the coastline, and the hostility of the natives, Dávila had little reason to doubt that Montejo and his people had come to grief. If that were true, then he had new responsibilities as the second in command, so he abandoned the attempt to reach Chactemal and made the arduous trek back to Salamanca de Xelha to rejoin the forces that he had left there. There he learned that no one had heard anything about the fate of Montejo.

The *adelantado*, meanwhile, was very much alive and still anchored offshore from the town of Chetumal, fending off the occasional assault by native warriors in canoes. As the Spanish waited, they watched the Maya strengthen their fortifications, including well-disguised pits to block any attack by men on horseback, a tactic that suggests knowledge of European warfare. Before long, Montejo received word through native informants that Dávila's contingent had been killed by hostile elements and native attacks. Following this shocking news, the Chactemal Maya surprisingly seemed to abandon hostilities and, in gestures of friendship, provided the Spanish party with foods such as maize, squash, and fowl. In Chamberlain's view, this apparent goodwill was part of a stratagem, likely devised by Guerrero, to induce Montejo, now faced with the loss of any land support, to leave the Bahía de Chetumal.[13]

The scheme was successful, and Montejo sailed away, not north but south to explore the coastline along Honduras. From there, he returned up the coast of Yucatán to Salamanca de Xelha, which he found deserted, seeming evidence that the remainder of his original forces had perished. On Cozumel, however, he was overjoyed to learn that Dávila had survived and, on his return to Salamanca de Xelha, had moved the town north to Xamanha, near the present site of Playa del Carmen, and called it Salamanca. Although Montejo still saw the Chactemal region as the best location for a colony, he desperately needed new men and supplies, so he sailed around Yucatán to Veracruz, leaving Dávila in charge of Salamanca de Xamanha. The Maya of Chactemal had bought themselves some time, and Guerrero was able to enjoy a relatively peaceful life with his family for another few years.

The next assault on Chactemal was launched in 1531, and it came from a surprising direction. Montejo had arrived in Veracruz in the summer of 1528 and by December was fully resupplied for the return to the Chactemal region. Before he could set sail, however, he was granted authority over the province of Tabasco, which he decided to use as a base from which to approach Chactemal across the peninsula from the west. With his son, also called Francisco de Montejo and known as El Mozo ("The Younger"), as a lieutenant, and with Dávila and his forces recalled from Salamanca de Xamanha, he began a campaign to gain control of Tabasco, much of which he achieved by early 1530. Then, as a result of the kind of political machinations that lay behind so much of the governance of the Spanish colonies, Tabasco was taken away from Montejo, and he was forced to find a different site from which to conquer and control Yucatán. This he found farther north along the west coast of the peninsula at the native town of Campeche, which, of course, he immediately named Salamanca de Campeche. From there, over the following decade, he directed a two-prong operation, dispatching a force to the northeast led by his son and another under Dávila southeast across the peninsula to Chactemal.

Dávila left Salamanca de Campeche with about fifty men, a native interpreter, and the *adelantado*'s young nephew, called like his uncle and cousin Francisco de Montejo. The party worked its way laboriously through the jungle toward Chactemal, meeting little resistance and surprisingly benign responses from the natives. Many of the tribes, it seemed to Dávila, chafed under the control exercised over them by Nachan Ka'an's Chactemal Maya and were prepared to assist him. Nachan Ka'an, however, remained defiant, responding to an overture for peace from Dávila by saying that "they preferred war and would give [them tribute of] fowls in the form of their lances and maize in the form of their arrows."[14] Despite this threat, when the Spanish party worked its way across Lake Bacalar, down a river to the Bahía de Chetumal, and along the coast to Chactemal, they were astonished to find the well-fortified town completely deserted. Nachan Ka'an's tribe, with Guerrero and his family, had abandoned their homes, their temples, and their fields and melted into the jungle.

Dávila took possession of Chactemal and liked what he saw. Like Montejo, he saw the town and the surrounding region as the most favourable site in Yucatán for the colony's principal settlement, and he established a new town called Villa Real, assigning its residents *encomienda*s carved out of the neighbouring land. Two months later, however, word reached Dávila that Nachan Ka'an's warriors had gathered at Chequitaquil, a town about ten kilometres up the coast and, with Guerrero likely at the helm, were preparing to attack Villa Real. In a pre-emptive strike, Dávila's soldiers approached silently in canoes one night, infiltrated the encampment, and routed the Maya in a surprise attack at dawn. It was a great victory, a battle that had seemingly smashed the Chactemal Maya, but when Dávila searched among the enemy dead and the more than sixty prisoners he could not find the two adversaries whom he was most desperate to destroy: Nachan Ka'an and Guerrero. When Dávila asked the prisoners about the whereabouts of the renegade Spaniard, he was told that he was dead.

Once again, as he had done with Cortés and Montejo, Guerrero had eluded the grasp of Dávila. Contrary to what the Mayan captives claimed, Guerrero was very much alive and, in Chamberlain's view, still Nachan Ka'an's military leader. The home base of the Chactemal Maya might have fallen into the hands of the Spanish, but within weeks widespread opposition began to develop all over the southern part of Yucatán. When Dávila moved inland to put the *encomienda* system in place and to remind the various *caciques* that they were required to pay tribute, he discovered a well-coordinated uprising, one that had spread all across the peninsula, even to Salamanca de Campeche. The tribes that had greeted him peaceably on his trek across to Chetumal had been roused to rebellion by something or someone; all of them were allied with the Chactemal tribe and were determined to drive the Spanish out of their lands.

Dávila faced a dilemma. Seemingly endless battles against enemy warriors had killed a number of his soldiers and horses and exhausted the rest. There would soon be little left with which to defend Villa Real from the attack certain to come. He had hoped for reinforcements from Campeche, but six soldiers whom he had sent with messages to Montejo were slaughtered as they made their way through the jungle. Subsequent attempts to have dispatches relayed by native carriers came to nothing as seemingly cooperative *caciques* promised help and then ordered the letters destroyed. Once again Dávila and Montejo were completely isolated from each other—indeed neither knew whether the other was still alive—and Dávila's position was precarious. By the autumn of 1532, with Villa

Real effectively blockaded, he decided to abandon the town and, like Montejo four years earlier, head down the coast to seek refuge in a Spanish settlement in Honduras. The church in Villa Real was taken apart, the Christian crosses were removed, and, in thirty-two canoes seized from the natives, Dávila's party was chased out of the Bahía de Chetumal by triumphant Mayan warriors.

Villa Real ceased to exist, Guerrero's Chactemal Maya reclaimed their town, and they were able to live free of the threat of Spanish intrusion for another twelve years. At Campeche, the *adelantado* quelled the rebellion that threatened to push him out of Yucatán, and he directed his attention to taking control of the northern part of the peninsula. In 1533, Montejo the Younger captured the important city of Chichén Itzá, but a year later he was driven from it by defiant natives, and within months both the *adelantado* and El Mozo had left Yucatán with their forces. By 1535, apart from a few Franciscan friars persistently seeking converts, there was not a single Spaniard on the peninsula. Except, of course, for Guerrero.

For the next five years, the Montejos directed their attention elsewhere, the father to gaining control of Honduras, over which he was given authority in 1535, and the son to governing Tabasco in his name. In the summer of 1540, when the *adelantado* turned again to the task of conquering and pacifying Yucatán, he was nearly seventy years of age and exhausted from years of struggle, so he gave the job to El Mozo. The son returned to Salamanca de Campeche with a substantial force and, aided by dissension among the Mayan tribes, was soon able to conquer the northern and western areas of the peninsula. In 1542, he created the city of Mérida on the site of the Mayan town of T'hó, and a year later the town of Valladolid was created in northeastern Yucatán out of materials plundered from Zaci, the Mayan town over which it was constructed.

Having gained a measure of control over the northern region of Yucatán, El Mozo decided on a third attempt to subdue the natives of the south, particularly those in Chactemal. In April 1543, he commissioned Gaspar Pacheco to establish a town in the region of the Bahía de Chetumal; however, when Pacheco became ill after a few months, command of the expedition was given to his son Melchor and nephew Alonso. Commandeering large quantities of maize and other foods, as well as natives from already subdued tribes to serve as porters, the Pacheco cousins headed south and soon found the Maya there as determined as ever to defend their homeland. As Montejo and Dávila had discovered before them, it was a terrain of rivers, lakes, marshes, and lagoons that impeded movement and gave an advantage to the natives, who knew how to manoeuvre through them. The Spanish, moreover, were confronted by the familiar pattern of abandonment of towns as the natives destroyed their crops and vanished into the jungle to conduct guerrilla warfare.

But destruction of the crops starved the Chactemal Maya as much as it did the Spanish, and the battle became one of attrition in which both sides became weakened and exhausted. In the Pachecos, the Maya faced enemies more ruthless and vicious than anything previously known in New Spain, even in the sometimes brutal campaigns of Cortés, Montejo, and Dávila. So savage were the actions of Alonso Pacheco that a Franciscan friar, Lorenzo de Bienvenida, complained of them in a letter written a few years later, on February 10, 1548, to the Spanish court:

> Nero was not more cruel than this man. He passed forward and reached a province called Chetumal, which was at peace. Even though the natives did not make war, he robbed the province and consumed the foodstuffs of the natives, who fled into the bush in fear of the Spanish, since as soon as [this captain] captured any of them, he set the dogs on them. And the Indians fled from all this and did not sow their crops, and all died of hunger. I say all, because there were pueblos of five hundred and one thousand houses, and now one which has one hundred is large. The province was also rich in cacao. This captain...with his own hands

committed outrages: he killed many with the garrote, saying, "This is a good rod with which to punish these people,"
and, after he had killed them, he said, "Oh how well I fin-
ished them off." Tying them to stakes, he cut the breasts off
many women, and hands, noses, and ears off the men, and
he tied squashes to the feet of women, and threw them in
the lakes to drown merely to amuse himself. He committed
other great cruelties which I shall not mention for lack of
space. He destroyed the entire province.[15]

Largely because the Maya were driven from the land that had
sustained them, abandoning their crops or burning them to prevent the Spanish from seizing them, they were unable to continue
the guerrilla warfare that had driven away both Montejo and
Dávila. Confronted by the cruel behaviour of the Pachecos, the
Maya no longer had the will to maintain a sustained resistance,
and they no longer seemed to have leaders to inspire them and
provide strategies to counteract the Spanish incursion. And, for
the first time in twenty-five years, they went into battle against
their invaders without Guerrero.

The disappearance from Yucatán and ultimate end of Guerrero
remain a mystery today. His last known contact with the Spanish
is thought to be his reply to Montejo's letter in 1528. Four years
later Dávila was told by local natives that Guerrero was dead, but
Chamberlain and other historians are convinced that this was a
ruse devised to confuse the Spanish, and the strategies employed
by the Chactemal Maya in that campaign suggest that Guerrero
was still a captain under Nachan Ka'an. In 1543, however, the
Pachecos heard nothing of him, and they faced none of the clever
and effective tactics that had thwarted Montejo and Dávila.

The answer to the question of the disappearance of Guerrero
likely lies not in the history of Yucatán but in that of Honduras to
the south. For a dozen years after the Cortés expedition there in
1524, rival factions of Spaniards had tried to colonize Honduras

but met with determined opposition from the indigenous people. In 1536, when the colony's acting governor, Andrés de Cerezeda, was ailing and had lost control of the colony, Pedro de Alvarado was sent in from Guatemala to subdue the natives. Alvarado was an experienced conquistador, having been second in command in the Cortés occupation of Tenochtitlán, and he was well known for his brutality, having ordered the slaughter of Aztec nobles during his leader's absence from the city. Ambitious and ruthless, he saw the chaos in Honduras as a chance to add more authority to his governorship of Guatemala.

Alvarado's particular target in Honduras was a powerful *cacique* named Ciçumba, who had resisted the Spanish for a dozen years and by the summer of 1536 had rallied a number of other native leaders around him. Ciçumba's rule stretched over a large part of the fertile lower reaches of the Río de Ulúa, a broad river originating high in the mountains of the interior and flowing into the Gulf of Honduras. His unrelenting harassment of the Spanish had led to the near abandonment of Cerezeda's base of operations, the optimistically named Villa de Buena Esperanza, located 110 kilometres inland. Positioned in a large and well-protected fortress on the banks of the Río de Ulúa, and commanding many hundreds of warriors, Ciçumba stood resolutely in the way of any colonial development.

Never one to resist a challenge, Alvarado decided to attack Ciçumba at his greatest strength, his fortress, and he sent his men onto the river for a bold assault by canoe. In a fierce battle, the Spanish overwhelmed and dispersed the native warriors and captured many of the tribal leaders who had joined Ciçumba. He himself was taken prisoner but allowed to live when he agreed to become a Christian and to live quietly with a small number of followers. His defeat turned out to be a decisive point in the Spanish conquest of the region: native resistance collapsed, and Alvarado took control of the western part of Honduras.

In the aftermath of the victory over Ciçumba, the Spanish made a remarkable discovery. Among the many natives lying dead

on the battlefield was a warrior dressed in Mayan clothing, covered with the traditional war paint, and wearing the ear plugs and
nose rings of the Maya. But he was not a Maya. In a letter to the
Spanish crown written at Puerto de Caballos on August 14, 1536,
Cerezeda reported that

> the *cacique* Ciçumba declared that during the combat which
> had taken place within the *albarrada* ["defensive barricade"]
> the day before a Christian Spaniard named Gonzalo Aroça
> had been killed by a shot from an arquebus. He is the one
> who lived among the Indians of the province of Yucatan for
> twenty years or more, and in addition is the one whom they
> say brought ruin to the *Adelantado* Montejo. And when that
> province had been abandoned by the Christians he came
> with a fleet of fifty canoes to aid the natives of this province
> to destroy those of us who were here. This was about five or
> six months before the arrival of the *Adelantado* (Alvarado),
> at the time when I executed certain *caciques*, as I have
> indicated above, on being informed of the treacherous con-
> spiracy with respect to peace negotiations which they had
> plotted. This Spaniard who was killed was nude, his body
> decorated, and he wore Indian dress.[16]

The Spanish chroniclers of the sixteenth century and most historians since then have accepted that the body on the battlefield
was that of Gonzalo Guerrero. Some, recalling that Cortés could
not pick out Aguilar from among several natives after his seven
years of captivity, have argued that a Spaniard who had lived as a
Maya for twenty-four years would be indistinguishable from the
other native dead. However, though Spanish eyes likely would not
have identified Guerrero, those of Ciçumba and the other natives
would have spotted him as a very unusual Maya. Unless Cerezeda
was fabricating another episode in the legend of the apostate
Spaniard in order to enhance the significance of Alvarado's victory,

Guerrero's life ended when the arquebus ball crashed into his skull on the banks of the Río de Ulúa.

If Guerrero died in Honduras, then it was as a warrior, not defending his home at Chactemal but on a battlefield many kilometres away. We will never know what impelled him to join the battles of other tribes against incursions by his former countrymen, but there are several possibilities. The simplest explanation is the self-interest of Nachan Ka'an and other Yucatán *caciques* who had long conducted lucrative trade and commerce with the coastal communities in Honduras and maintained agents and trading posts in the region. The threat to this productive enterprise might well have led Nachan Ka'an to deploy his chief *nacom* and several hundred of his best fighting men to assist Ciçumba in his resistance to Spanish conquest.

A more interesting possibility is suggested by Cerezeda's letter: Guerrero, the conqueror of Montejo and Dávila, had become so renowned among both the Spanish and the natives that he could not refuse the call to lead another resistance. Had the departure of every Spaniard from Yucatán in 1535 deceived his *cacique*, his tribe, and Gonzalo himself into believing that guerrilla warfare could drive the intruders away forever? The natives would have expected him to lead them to victory in Honduras, as he had in Yucatán, and he might have come to expect it of himself. Was he, like a protagonist in a Joseph Conrad novel, consumed by the public role that circumstances had thrust on him so that the private man, with a wife and family, was pushed aside? Or had he, like a classically tragic figure, come to believe in his own invincibility, that nothing, not even Spanish steel and gunpowder, could kill him?

And what of Zazil Há and Mexico's first *mestizo* children? Following Guerrero's death, the Chactemal Maya had seven years without external threat until the Pachecos invaded southern Yucatán in 1543. By then, Guerrero's sons would have been old enough to be warriors, and they might well have fought and died in the vicious battles that ensued. All members of the family would have suffered from the dislocation of their tribe and from the widespread starvation caused by the loss of land on which to plant crops and by the seizure of any remaining foods by the Spanish. As Chamberlain has observed,

> the inexorable conquest, occupation, and organization of their lands by the Spanish inevitably created chaos within the structure of Maya society and made necessary a long period of recuperation and readjustment. The extent to which the fabric of native life was torn apart in the several cacicazgos ["tribal regions"] of Yucatan varied in proportion to the resistance they had offered. It was, of course, much greater in the provinces which had carried on a desperate struggle for existence than in those which had submitted readily.... Indeed Uaymil-Chetumal is said to have suffered irrevocable ruin as a result of the campaign of the Pachecos, and it never thereafter assumed its former important position or anything near its former population.[17]

In the face of the barbarity of the Pachecos and the destruction of their home, their tribal autonomy, their farms, and their commercial trade, Zazil Há and her children likely joined the exodus of several thousand Maya from the southernmost parts of Yucatán and melted into the jungle. Many of their tribe migrated southwest into the interior and settled around Lake Petén, the only region available to Yucatán Maya who did not wish to live under Spanish control. Deep in the jungle, they and their descendants were able to maintain their political independence and practise their religion for another 175 years. Some of the migrants eventually returned to the Chetumal area, but it never regained the vitality, power, and influence that it had enjoyed under Nachan Ka'an and his Spanish/Mayan *nacom.*

The fate of Zazil Há and her children will never be known. There is a good chance, though, that there are *mestizos* now living on the Yucatán Peninsula—or elsewhere in Mexico—who carry the DNA of Guerrero within them. In a nation comprising 60 per cent *mestizos*, they would share a unique heritage: a lineage that stretches back through 500 years to the moment when a new people was created in Mexico by the union of a European father and an indigenous mother. But others who do not carry the Guerrero DNA might well have inherited something else from the man: the renegade mentality.

With the Pachecos' occupation of the Uaymil-Chetumal region, and the suppression of a Mayan revolt in 1546, the Montejo family finally had control of the Yucatán Peninsula. Making Mérida their headquarters, they erected their cathedral, a massive structure to embody the domination of the new religion; and, to represent their own political and military supremacy, they built a grand house in Mérida's central square, the elaborate façade of which still survives. Prominent over the doorway are two large figures of Spanish halberdiers whose boots are resting on the anguished heads of the vanquished, either traditional European symbols of the defeated or more specific representations of the vanquished Maya.

More than 200 years later, on December 14, 1761, the Montejo halberdiers were still looking balefully out on Mérida's plaza, where a charismatic Mayan leader who called himself Jacinto Canek was being tortured, dismembered, and burned. Eight other leaders were hanged, and many of their native followers were given the lash and had limbs cut off in reprisal for their attempted rebellion. The truth is that, despite their brutal treatment at the hands of the Spanish, the Maya of the Yucatán Peninsula had never been fully subjugated, and they would continue to fight for independence through the Caste War of the nineteenth century and into the twentieth century. It was a battle that began when Gonzalo Guerrero became a Mayan warrior, and it was a struggle for which he gave his life.

CHAPTER EIGHT

"The Power of Narrative Is Absolute": GUERRERO IN THE CONTEMPORARY MEXICAN CONSCIOUSNESS

I n the nearly five centuries following the death of Gonzalo Guerrero, his story has been recorded, embellished, reinterpreted, and refashioned. The unstable border between history and fiction, between fact and folklore, and the inevitable mythologizing that develops around extraordinary historical figures have made Guerrero a legend and an icon. He shares this position with more prominent figures of the conquest period of Mexican history—Hernán Cortés and Malinche—though their stories are more securely founded upon archival documentation. Even his fellow castaway, Jerónimo de Aguilar, has become the subject of speculation, mythologizing, and valorization. Moreover, with the passage of time, the iconic meanings of these figures, particularly Cortés and Malinche, for many Mexicans have overlapped that of Guerrero. The Spanish/Mayan father/warrior has come out of the shadows to provide an important perspective on the creation of the majority of Mexican people: the *mestizos*.

Sixteenth-century Spanish chroniclers, notably Bernal Díaz del Castillo and Francisco López de Gómara, celebrated Cortés as the conqueror of the Aztecs, a heroic figure who had secured a huge new territory and many new subjects for his king and country. When the protracted War of Independence made Mexico free of Spain in 1821, however, Cortés was seen from a much different perspective. For many Mexicans, particularly the growing body of *mestizos*, he was a brutal conqueror who had tried to destroy the cultures and beliefs of the country's indigenous peoples. Fears that his body, interred in a mausoleum attached to the Church and Hospital of Jesus that he had founded in Mexico City, would be desecrated led to its relocation, along with a statue and his coat of arms, at a less prominent site. In 1882, a plan to place his bones alongside those of heroes of the War of Independence angered people and led to an attempt to damage his tomb. The remains of Cortés were essentially hidden until 1947, when they were rediscovered and reburied in the hospital, but placing a copy of a bust of him there in 1981 sparked yet another attempt at desecration.

One of the most famous and savage attacks on Cortés came from the brush of the distinguished Mexican muralist Diego Rivera in his fresco *Colonial Domination*. Completed in the National Palace in Mexico City in 1951, and based upon suppositions about the physical appearance of Cortés made from an examination of his bones, Rivera's portrait was that of "an emaciated, hunchbacked, syphilitic, and degenerate man."[1] Rarely has the "founder" of a nation been treated with such contempt.

If the scorn of many twentieth-century Mexicans had been directed at a man known only as a ruthless foreign destroyer of a rich culture and civilization, then it would have been a straightforward matter of indigenous hatred of an enemy invader. But when the name of Cortés is linked with that of Malinche, as inevitably it is, the situation becomes much more complex. The past century saw the conquistador's Nahuatl translator herself become an object of contempt because of the essential role that she played in his conquest of the Aztecs. Viewed as a traitor to her people, an opportunist who betrayed them to their enemy, she spawned the common pejorative term *malinchista*, which initially meant "traitor" but has become softened to denote someone who prefers all things foreign. Her role has also sparked a large body of literature, and Mexican and Mexican American feminist scholars have offered several defences of her role in the conquest. Some commentators have argued that Malinche was a victim who had no choice but to collaborate with Cortés: she became his property when given to him by her own people, and as such she had no option but to serve as his translator and mistress. Others have gone further, portraying her as a shrewd, highly capable woman who thrived in the difficult situation into which she had been thrust. In their view, she demonstrated great skill as an interpreter and adviser on native customs, beliefs, and ways of thinking, and she survived her captivity and eventual discarding by Cortés.

Like Cortés, Malinche would have evoked fairly uncomplicated antipathy from twentieth-century Mexicans if she had been simply a collaborator who had aided a military conquest. But when she bore Cortés a son, one who did not fade into obscurity in the countryside but went on to be recognized as the conquistador's offspring, albeit illegitimate, she became recognized as much more than a mere translator and military resource. She was seen as the mother of the country's first *mestizo*, one half of the founding parentage of Mexico, at first only a symbolic designation since the birth of Martín Cortés in 1524 was clearly not the first of a child of European and indigenous parents.

Martín was accorded the title of first Mexican *mestizo*, according to Sandra Messinger Cypess, a professor of Latin American literature at the University of Maryland, for political and cultural reasons based upon the social standing of his father: "He is the first in social rank as the son of a conquistador, and his Catholic religion, dress, and journey to Spain...all prove male dominance over Amerindian women and European cultural dominance over

Amerindian ways of life."[2] As time went by, this symbolic designation was proclaimed often enough that it came to be mistaken as historical fact.

Malinche's identity as the mother of the *mestizos*, according to Octavio Paz and other commentators, has haunted much of the Mexican population for more than a generation. If Cortés and Malinche are the original parents of the race—its Adam and Eve—then *mestizos* are bastards, the offspring of the rape of an indigenous woman by a foreign, colonizing man. So strongly held was this view, especially among younger Mexicans, that, when a statue of Cortés, Malinche, and Martín called *Monumento al mestizaje* was commissioned in 1982, it met with fierce opposition. Placed in the main square of Coyoacán, near where they had lived in the years following the fall of Tenochtitlán, it portrayed the conquistador (modelled on the Spanish Mexican actor Germán Robles) standing authoritatively, with Malinche seated as if on a throne beside him. Martín, perhaps only five years old, stood as commandingly as his father, his arm extended as he pointed into the distance, presumably into Mexico's future. There was no suggestion, of course, of the real future that the boy and his mother faced at the side of Cortés: she to be handed off to one of his lieutenants and he to spend the rest of his life in the shadow of his legitimate half-brother. In the eyes of many people, the statue was a misrepresentation of history and an affront, and the resulting protests forced its removal to a little-known park in Churubusco, a suburb of Mexico City. Perhaps not surprisingly, vandals have since removed the figure of Martín from the site.

Ignored in the Mexican obsession with Cortés and Malinche, of course, is another paradigm of founding parentage: that of Guerrero, Zazil Há, and their children. Guerrero has always been a shadowy figure, seen as perhaps more legend than real man, whereas Cortés, through his own writing and that of many others, is firmly grounded in history. He is, moreover, the conquistador who brought down an empire, whereas Guerrero's abilities as a warrior, alluded to in various chronicles, were directed against the Spanish invaders. Cortés undertook his campaigns in the heart of Mexico against the great city of Tenochtitlán and the Aztec emperor Montezuma, whereas Guerrero engaged in jungle skirmishes in the remote and little-valued Yucatán. And, no less significantly, the mother of the *mestizo* son of Cortés became a well-known figure in her own right, whereas Guerrero's wife slipped into the jungle and obscurity. It is hardly surprising, then, that Cortés and Malinche have been seen as Mexico's founding family.

Although always much less widely known than Cortés, Guerrero has fared much better in public opinion in Mexico in the twentieth and twenty-first centuries. While the conquistador was falling from the lofty heights at which he had been placed by sixteenth-century chroniclers, the Spanish/Mayan castaway began to be viewed differently from the figure described by those chroniclers. This change came about not because new evidence was brought to bear on the Guerrero story, but because it was being seen through a new lens, that of the changing nature of Mexican society and the evolving attitudes of its people to the *mestizo*.

For various reasons, the Spaniards of the sixteenth century, in control of the historical narrative through the work of its chroniclers, damned Guerrero in the strongest terms. To Gonzalo Fernández de Oviedo, he was of "vile caste," the product of "vile heretics," a "bad Christian," a "traitor and apostate sailor," an "infidel mariner," and "a bad Christian transformed into an Indian."[3] To Diego de Landa, he was "an idolater" who had descended to decorating his body, growing his hair, and wearing rings in his pierced ears. Bernal Díaz del Castillo seemingly gave no such moral judgment in his version of Aguilar's report to Cortés that Guerrero, having married a native woman, had tattooed his face and pierced his lower lip. To Spanish readers of his time, however, Díaz del Castillo needed to say no more: mutilation of the body and cohabitation with an indigenous woman were considered abominations. Francisco López de Gómara made this more explicit by having Aguilar attribute Guerrero's refusal to join Cortés to "shame...because his nose and ears had been pierced, and his face and hands painted in the manner of that country and people, and also because of his attachment to his wife and love of his children."[4] Francisco Cervantes de Salazar's *Crónica de la Nueva España*, written about 1566 but not published until the nineteenth century, characterized this attachment as "the vice he had committed with the woman."[5]

The shame reported by the sixteenth- and seventeenth-century chroniclers reflected the Spanish attitudes of the time toward indigenous people and *mestizos*, expressed in their most extreme form by the Spanish philosopher and theologian Juan Ginés de Sepúlveda. In Valladolid in 1550 (without ever having been to the New World), he engaged Bartolomé de las Casas (who had spent years in New Spain) in an important public debate about the rights and treatment of Spain's newly colonized peoples. Ginés de Sepúlveda argued that the conquest and enslavement of the inhabitants of America were legitimate because they were inferior to Spaniards. Without a true society, they had no property and therefore no rights, and incapable of reason they could not be converted to Spanish culture and religion. The severity of this assessment of the indigenous people ensured that, when Ginés de Sepúlveda wrote his *Historia del Nuevo Mundo* in 1562, he too saw great shame in Guerrero's adoption of Mayan life and his fathering of mixed-race offspring. It was a belief reiterated in the works of early-seventeenth-century Spanish writers, notably Antonio de Herrera y Tordesilla's *Historia de los Hechos de los Castellanos en las islas i Tierra Firme del Mar Oceano* (1601) and Juan de Torquemada's *Los veinte i un libros rituales y monarchia Indiana* (1615). And it was an idea that remained unchanged for more than three centuries.

The reinterpretation of Guerrero in Mexico in the late twentieth century resulted in part from a changing attitude toward *mestizaje*. According to Mexican social historian Moisés González

Navarro, most of the unions between indigenous people and those of Spanish descent over the centuries were illegitimate, making the term "*mestizo*" synonymous with "bastard," a stigma that began to disappear only after the Mexican Revolution of 1910–20 began to rehabilitate indigenous culture.[6] It was, however, a thorny issue that remained residually embedded in the Mexican psyche, and as late as 1950 Paz could make it the foundation of his first articulation of *The Labyrinth of Solitude*.

Guerrero is absent from Paz's discussion of Mexico's *mestizo* origins, and he is largely ignored in the writing of one of the country's other eminent public intellectuals, Carlos Fuentes. In 1992, Fuentes wrote that Malinche "established the basis of our multiracial civilization. She bore the child of the conqueror, the first mestizo, the first American of mixed blood. She was symbolically the mother of the first Mexican, the first child of Indian and Spanish blood."[7] When he examined the conquest in two of the five novellas in *El Naranjo, o los círculos del tiempo* (*The Orange Tree*) a year later, Fuentes was little interested in Guerrero. "Sons of the Conquistador" is narrated by the two Martín Cortéses: the *mestizo* son of Malinche and the legitimate son of Hernán's Spanish wife. "The Two Shores," recounted from beyond the grave by Aguilar shortly after his painful death from buboes, tells of his role as translator for Cortés, the fall of Tenochtitlán, and his jealousy at being supplanted at the conquistador's side by Malinche. Fuentes dramatically revises history by portraying Aguilar as a sympathizer with the Atzecs, one who falls under the spell of their culture and deliberately sabotages the Spanish efforts at subjugation. Guerrero is only a bit player in this account, appearing in the magic realist conclusion, in which Aguilar imagines the conquest in reverse, one in which Guerrero leads an army of Mayan and Caribbean fighters in an assault on Spain. A kind of avenging warrior/angel, this Gonzalo is "too busy fighting and conquering. He doesn't have time to tell stories.... He has to act, decide, order, punish."[8]

While Paz and Fuentes were placing Cortés, Malinche, and Aguilar at the centre of the conquest narrative, other writers were beginning to present an alternative history in which Guerrero is an important figure, perhaps even the central one. Two of these accounts were presented not as works of fiction but as long-buried but newly discovered memoirs of the Spanish castaway himself. The first, *Gonzalo de Guerrero, padre del mestizaje iberoamericano*, was published by journalist Mario Aguirre Rosas as a series of articles in the Mexico City newspaper *El Universal* in 1975.[9] Rosas claimed to have edited Guerrero's memoir, which he said was written on deerskin vellum obtained from the Montejo expedition and contained in thirty folios held by a private collector in Mexico City. Although this story echoes much of the work of the early chroniclers, it veers sharply away from it by presenting Guerrero as a native of Extremadura rather than Andalusia, and though he fights with the Maya he hopes that the Spanish will triumph. "The narrative," says scholar Roseanna Mueller, "is full of complications and ironies. It is an alternative view of history, with a suspiciously modern political message."[10]

The second set of Guerrero "memoirs" was published in Mérida in 1994 as part of a document titled *Historias de la conquista del Mayab, 1511–1697*. It is purported to be an account written in 1724–25 by a Franciscan friar, Joseph de San Buenaventura y Cartagena (a name that does not appear in the Franciscan records for the period), but discovered in Mexico City only in the early 1990s. As in the earlier "memoir," Guerrero's words were said to have been preserved on paper and deerhide. "I have these writings and skins with me," asserts the friar, "and it is a difficult task to verify and read. And from what I can read from these writings, this is what happened according to don Gonzalo de Guerrero."[11]

Unlike the protagonist of the 1975 "memoir"—and indeed the figure in the chronicles—this Guerrero is an upper-class man from Extremadura, and he even more intensely desires Spanish domination of the New World. He teaches his children the

Spanish language and is unhappy with the fierce guerrilla warfare of the Maya, in part because one of his sons fights with the guerrillas. Having retained his Catholicism, he believes that Spanish rule will quickly convert the Maya from worshipping their idols and following their barbaric customs because they are "by nature peaceful, free from wars of their own, and untainted by the vices and filthy habits that characterize other native groups."[12] That is, by yielding to Spanish domination the Maya can become civilized.

Although these supposed autobiographical documents provide interesting perspectives on the Guerrero story, their variations from the conventional historical accounts and the seeming influence of contemporary Mexican concerns with matters such as *mestizaje* have made scholars dismiss them as inauthentic memoirs. "The implausibility of both of these allegedly autobiographical accounts," says Rolena Adorno, "is patent. The authenticity of either manuscript is far from being proven, and the contents of both are enough steps removed from any potentially original account by Gonzalo as to inspire skepticism rather than confidence."[13]

A more conventional account of the Guerrero story appeared in one of twenty-five volumes of a historical series published in 1992 to coincide with the 500th anniversary of the arrival of Columbus in the New World. A hardcover comic book drawn by the Spanish illustrator Miguel Calatayud with some text by Fernando Savater, *Conquistadores en Yucatán: La desaparición de Gonzalo Guerrero* treats its protagonist as the father of Mexican *mestizaje* but emphasizes his role as a renegade warrior. It begins with his death at the hands of Pedro de Alvarado; recounts his battles with Hernández de Córdoba, Montejo, and Dávila; and ends with an ambiguous appraisal of his role: "We will never know the truth. A renegade to some, a hero of legends for others, what was his real role in this madness?"[14]

In the absence of authentic new archival material, a number of authors have inevitably turned to fiction as a way to flesh out the bare bones of the story related by the sixteenth-century chroniclers. The first, and most acclaimed, of these accounts is Eugenio Aguirre's *Gonzalo Guerrero*, a "historical novel" published in Mexico in 1980. Consisting of ten chapters, most of which are narrated by Guerrero, it tells of his days in Darién, the shipwreck and capture by the Maya, his life as a slave and rise to prominence in his tribe, his marriage to the chief's daughter (here called Ix Chel Can), his resistance to the Spanish incursion into Yucatán, and his death in 1536. The story is grounded on the historical accounts and legends (contained in an extensive bibliography), but with the freedom of a novelist Aguirre imagines a fuller narrative. Most notably, he envisages an episode in which Guerrero, deeply inculcated with Mayan religious beliefs, attempts to appease the gods by sacrificing his daughter Ix Mo at the famous *cenote* at Chichén Itzá.

Aguirre's novel was innovative in 1980 because it foregrounds Guerrero, inverting the conventional idea of him as a traitor and presenting him as a heroic figure. It also presents a sympathetic view of the indigenous cultures, concluding with an elaborate tribute to the Spanish castaway's role in the creation of the *mestizo*:

> In the legend, his name remains blood star, blond gem, that came to create a melting pot of a new race, a new lineage, the cosmic adventure of the new peoples; bird that nested in the tanned bed of the dark skin of the Mayab to engender the ancillary customs of the young culture of America. Let song rise in your honour, let the trail of the jungle be blazed, the gods be perfumed with incense. They who guided your steps and who opened their sanctuaries to receive your offering, the gifts of an old world which spilled blood and ashes to sketch the profile of these lands, of these men who now belatedly honour you and engrave your name Gonzalo Guerrero or Gonzalo de Aroca or Gonzalo Marinero, with deep pride in the parchment of their conscience.[15]

Gonzalo Guerrero has been praised for its amplification of the Guerrero legend and its challenge to the criteria by which historic figures are identified as heroes or traitors. At the same time, scholars and critics have pointed out that Aguirre makes the Spaniard the dominant contributor to the *mestizaje* that occurred in the union of Guerrero and his Mayan wife. Remaining a Catholic to the end, he adopts Mayan religious practices insofar as they help him to achieve prominence in his tribe, and it is his military expertise, not the valour and tactics of the indigenous warriors, that stymies the Spanish for so long. Thus, says Mark A. Hernández, the novel "remythifies him as a hero of the Mexican people, without fundamentally altering the asymmetrical power relations between the superior Spaniards and the 'inferior' indigenous populations in the ideology of *mestizaje*."[16]

A different view of Guerrero's role in Mexican *mestizaje* is taken up in Otilio Meza's 1994 novel *Un amor inmortal: Gonzalo Guerrero, símbolo del origen del mestizaje mexicano (novela histórica)*. The author of a series of romantic stories about historic figures of the conquest, Meza asserts that Guerrero's story is "unbeknownst to many Mexicans."[17] She focuses on the love of Guerrero for his Mayan wife and children, suggesting that it was the making of a new man, one who found a richer and more satisfying life in his Mayan community than he would have experienced in joining Cortés and returning to Spain.

Meza's novel was followed a year later by Mexican journalist Carlos Villa Roiz's *Gonzalo Guerrero: Memoria olvidada, trauma de México*, most of which is told by Guerrero's *mestiza* daughter. Like Aguirre, Villa Roiz uses the early chronicles—and some twentieth-century histories—but reinterprets them to make the Spanish castaway the protagonist. The narrator explains that she is recording her father's story to pre-empt those who will provide a "*versión triunfalista*": that is, a version of history fabricated by the triumphant and dominant Spanish:

Victors impose their customs and history.

In writing my father's biography I do him justice because those who do not record their memories risk others inventing them, and this is what the conquistadors are doing, by writing their triumphalist version of the crimes they committed. In this book, I include some pages where my father recorded events; things forgotten.... Guerrero, more than a surname, is a symbol.[18]

According to Villa Roiz, the imposition of Catholicism and Spanish culture on Mexico has done great damage to the religious foundations of the indigenous people: "The profoundly religious indigenous world has fallen into hypocrisy and secrecy. The truth has become sectarian, occultist. This is the trauma of all Mexico, the forgotten memory; they have forced us to lie, to hide our beliefs and feelings, to condemn what is ours and glorify what is foreign."[19] Thus, Guerrero's daughter, who began her account by declaring that "I am *mestiza* but I consider myself an Indian," concludes with elegiac acceptance of her parentage and mixed-blood heritage: "I seek myself inside his story, I find memories; to learn more about myself. I need to see myself reflected in others and the best mirror to understand my *mestizo* blood, the first one in this part of the world, is the life of my father: Gonzalo Guerrero."[20]

The Guerrero story has been reimagined by creative writers in the United States and Europe, some of whose work has been published and performed in Mexico. In 1999, the American artist and author Alan Clark published two plays for voices as *Guerrero and Heart's Blood* in Mexico.[21] The first, narrated by Guerrero, his Mayan wife, his father-in-law Nachancan, and Aguilar, emphasizes Guerrero's transformation as a Mayan warrior by focusing on his initiation into human sacrifice and ritual cannibalism. In the second, Aguilar provides a more conventional account of their shipwreck, his life as a slave, and Guerrero's rejection of the chance to join Cortés.

Another American author, John Curl, included "Homage to Gonzalo Guerrero" in his *Scorched Birth: Poems*, published in California in 2004.[22] Much of it is a simple retelling of the story from the chronicles, celebrating the Spanish renegade's military leadership and his death as a hero in Honduras. The English writer Anita Mason's 2011 novel *The Right Hand of the Sun* is largely about Aguilar, who narrates much of it, and his travels with Cortés. A later section, though, deals with his relationship with Guerrero, whom he sees as a kind of cultural chameleon adjusting all too easily to Mayan life. "Once I lived in Palos," Guerrero tells his companion. "Then I lived on a ship. Now I live here."[23] Mason sensationalizes the relationship between the men when she describes Aguilar witnessing Guerrero engaged in sex with a Mayan boy and then being rejected when he offers himself by Guerrero because "you are a Spaniard."[24] Aguilar subsequently worries that this homosexuality could get them both killed by the Spanish, and this danger becomes the reason that he never passes on the message from Cortés to his friend.

The novel *Maya Lord*, by John Coe Robbins, published in the United States in 2011, is a much more historically accurate and conventional account of the shipwreck and the fates of Guerrero and Aguilar.[25] A novelist, scriptwriter, and documentary film producer, Robbins provides a vivid evocation of sixteenth-century Yucatán and the clash of European and New World cultures. Aware of the dramatic possibilities of the tale, he focuses on the contrasting attitudes toward the plights of the two castaways and on their divergent careers.

The works of Clark, Curl, Mason, and Robbins have been aimed primarily at English-speaking readers outside Mexico and have had little impact inside that country. Much more likely to be influential is Alfonso Mateo-Sagasta's Spanish-language novel *Caminarás con el sol*, published in Barcelona in 2011 and distributed in Mexico. A novelist and historian, Mateo-Sagasta presents revisionist history in a balanced way, showing Guerrero beginning as a violent soldier in pursuit of gold and fame and being transformed into someone who respects both the Maya and their land. Sparked by a reunion with Aguilar late in his life, Guerrero narrates his story in three parts: "My Misfortune," "My Fortune," and "My Destiny." After describing his early days in Andalusia, he declares that "my second birth was in the Indies, only twenty years after Columbus saw the islands for the first time."[26] Guerrero's account of his life reflects his adoption of the Mayan idea of the circularity of time, and it acknowledges both his Spanish heritage and his rebirth:

> I have not forgotten that name was Gonzalo Guerrero and that I was born on the other side of the sea. Luckily, the same sea corrected my course, dropping me into the right place for me.
>
> To think that I was one of those who believed that the sky did not reach beyond Hercules' columns...! Perhaps those from here are right and time advances in circles, because nothing seems to me so far away and at the same time so near as the beginning of this story. It happens that I, when I only awaited death, was reborn.[27]

He calls his initial sight of the Maya "my first contact with the horror of these lands,"[28] but his later tender description of his first son being breastfed by his Mayan wife reveals how much he really has been reborn in New Spain. Unlike Aguilar and the other captive Spaniards, Guerrero is prepared to open himself to the life of the other, and he undergoes a genuine transformation.

Mateo-Sagasta clearly wants to revise the conventional Guerrero story and, beyond it, the broader history of the Spanish incursion into the New World. Although Guerrero was considered a traitor in his time, he says, "our perception of the world has changed. Today we understand the value of diversity, value the relationship with nature and that there is a different way to face the world."[29] In doing this, he—and to some degree Aguirre, Villa Roiz, and others—are part of a contemporary process taking place in South, Central, and North America. That process is the challenging of historical narratives imposed on the Americas by various European countries for political, social, and religious reasons. Victoria E. Campos describes the movement:

> Novelists like Homero Aridjis and Carmen Boullosa have chosen to dramatize the process of narrative and political exclusion. Returning to Spanish American colonial documents, Aridjis, Boullosa, and others collect historical material with which to retrospectively fictionalize the colonial past, but they also restructure the narrative by demonstrating how chroniclers used historiographic discourse to configure a present and a set of social relations convenient to themselves and the imperialist ambitions of the Spanish kings.[30]

Canadian essayist and novelist John Ralston Saul, in writing about the necessity of reshaping the historical narratives of his own country, those that have long been entrenched in school textbooks and university syllabuses, has asserted that "the power of narrative is absolute."[31] But altering a deeply embedded narrative is a long process, and the effect on a nation's attitudes toward cultural difference, diversity of viewpoints, and multiple historical influences can move with glacial speed. Thus, while some Mexican authors are offering provocative retellings of the Guerrero story, the public in their country is largely unaware of it and its potential as a *mestizaje* paradigm that challenges that of Cortés and Malinche. There are no statues of Guerrero outside the Yucatán Peninsula in Mexico (there are no memorials of Aguilar anywhere) and little acknowledgement of him in the country at large.

The story of Guerrero and his Mayan family remains very much a Yucatán one, celebrated on the peninsula for two reasons: partly because his resistance to Spanish domination reflects the Yucatán spirit of independence from the rest of Mexico, but more importantly because of the template that his story offers for the union of European and indigenous cultures. Public recognition of him and his Mayan family is met on the peninsula not with protests and vandalism, but with approval and pride.

The earliest celebration of Guerrero's role in *mestizaje*, the Ayala statue in Akumal, originated with a private citizen, but civic governments throughout the peninsula have increasingly promoted it publicly through statuary, street and district names, and various forms of art. Some people argue that such public memorializing is done simply to promote Yucatán tourism, but much of the commemoration is off the tourist track and clearly directed at local people. Early in the 1980s, the State of Quintana Roo commissioned a brief Spanish-language pamphlet titled *Gonzalo Guerrero: Apuntes para su biografía* (Gonzalo Guerrero: Notes for a Biography). In 1999, it funded a performance in Spanish and English, by the well-known Mexican actor Alejandro Reza, of Clark's *Heart's Blood* at Aktun Chen, in Quintana Roo.

Although Guerrero is celebrated in part for his defiance in the face of Spanish domination, public representations of him on the Yucatán Peninsula increasingly focus on his role in *mestizaje*. The magnificent Pacheco mural, commissioned by the government of the State of Yucatán for the Governor's Palace in Mérida in the 1970s, portrays a humble farmer with his Mayan wife and *mestizo* son. The mural by S. Cuevas painted for Mérida City Hall in 1978 is called *Origen del mestizaje* and carries this inscription: "Next to the robust Spaniard, lying beside him without submission, the Indian woman with languid gaze saw her companion arrive amidst the ocean waves, and their son, his eyes the color of corn and wheat, with the sorrow and the pride of mixed races." Several kilometres away, the entrance to the district of Mérida called Gonzalo Guerrero carries this legend: "Gonzalo Guerrero, Father of Mexican mestizaje. He fought and died defending the freedom of the Maya people."

As the Mexican Caribbean edition of *USA Today* has said, "the voice of that one man still echoes throughout the Maya territory nearly 500 years later."[32] Chetumal, the capital of Quintana Roo, proudly calls itself the "Cradle of *Mestizaje*," and a few kilometres away in Belize the National Institute of Archaeology in Santa Rita conducts re-enactments of the wedding of Guerrero and Zazil Há. A statue of them and their children, called the *Monument to the Cradle of Mestizaje*, stands prominently at the entrance to Chetumal, which in May 2016 launched its new Cradle of Mestizaje Museum. It would not have been out of place for the opening ceremonies to have included Mayan poet Ramón Iván Suárez Caamal's popular and frequently performed song "Hymn to Quintana Roo." Made the official state hymn in 1985, it honours the mixed heritage of so many of the people of the Yucatán Peninsula:

> This land facing east
> Cradle of the first miscegenation
> Love born without outrage
> Gonzalo Guerrero and Zazil.[33]

"Love born without outrage," a paradigm antithetical to the Cortés-Malinche union, has much to offer a country whose history, according to Paz, is one "of a man seeking his parentage, his origins."[34] Unfortunately, this is a truth recognized more quickly by American academics than by the average Mexican outside the Yucatán Peninsula. In 1992, Rolando Romero wrote that, even if much of the Guerrero story is mythical, it provides an attractive counterbalance to that of Cortés and Malinche, a different model that influenced even the dominant Spanish:

> Gonzalo Guerrero is thus proof that the encounter produced bilateral changes. Gonzalo Guerrero as a counter Malinche serves, in my opinion, as a new model of cultural syncretism. This model is based not on the violation and destruction

suggested by Paz's Malinche, but on the respect and the willing acceptance of the culture of the Other. Guerrero as a counter model to the conquest shows that the territory the Spanish found on their way to the Orient changed both the Old and the New World.[35]

In 2005, Sandra Messinger Cypess extended the argument for Guerrero in a scholarly essay on Malinche:

Documentation exists of another couple whose pattern of behavior subverts the supposed inferiority of the Amerindian culture that is read into the Malinche-Cortés relationship. Another cultural pattern can be symbolized by the behavior of an almost forgotten, emblematic couple, Gonzalo Guerrero and his Maya wife.... Guerrero's lifestyle and his adherence to his Maya wife and children deconstruct the dominant culture's view of the Amerindians as inferior, unworthy of loyalty and respect. In contrast to that of [the popular view of Cortés and Malinche], the pattern that Gonzalo Guerrero provides indicates that the European can reject aspects of his heritage in favor of the Amerindian pattern provided by the woman.... The historical presence of Gonzalo Guerrero offers us a paradigm in which the European male celebrates difference and contributes to diversity and pride of identity.[36]

As Romero and Cypess demonstrate, Guerrero belongs in any discussion of Malinche. If he represents an alternative to Cortés as a European male in New Spain, he also complements Malinche as a figure who stood in the middle of what Camilla Townsend calls "the drama of two continents colliding."[37] They were opposites in so many ways: he a European male thrust into the world of the Maya, she an indigenous woman compelled to adapt to the ethos and practices of an alien, invasive force. And their experiences were contrasting. Whereas Malinche's contributions to the conquest of the Aztecs only guaranteed her survival among the conquistadors and some consideration as the wife of one of them, Guerrero rose from slave to military leader and prominent member of his Mayan tribe. Malinche was part of the inexorable Spanish domination of Mexico, whereas Guerrero died on the battlefield in a vain attempt to prevent that supremacy from spreading throughout Yucatán and Central America. Even their places in history have undergone starkly contrasting changes. Whereas she went from being the valued instrument of Cortés in the first histories to the contemptible whore described by Paz, Guerrero's early reputation as a degenerate traitor became recast as the heroic opponent of Spanish hegemony.

As familiar as the Guerrero story is on the Yucatán Peninsula, it has only begun to move into the national consciousness. This is unfortunate because Guerrero and Zazil Há offer a paradigm in which the Old and New Worlds are joined without violence and exploitation, in which the patriarchal and narrow Eurocentric attitudes of at least one man were tempered by respect for the ways of life of the indigenous peoples. Guerrero was proud of the results of his union with Zazil Há: "Look how handsome these boys of mine are," he told Aguilar. The offspring of a marriage as legitimate as any blessed by the Catholic Church, they were not bastards, and they were not the results of exploitation and rape. They were surely worthy ancestors, if only symbolically, of the *mestizos* of modern Mexico.

"We Are a Métis Civilization"

I am a retired teacher of English literature, a professor emeritus who has devoted a long career to exploring the meaning, subtlety, and power of the literature of Great Britain and English North America. I have written and edited six books about William Somerset Maugham, a monograph about British authors employed in cultural propaganda during the Second World War, and a volume about a Canadian soldier who returned from enduring five years of that war and took his own life. I have even coauthored a social and cultural history of a Canadian football club. What, might you ask, led me to leave that familiar and relatively comfortable academic terrain and write about a Spanish sailor cast up on the Yucatán shore in the early sixteenth century? Why spend years finding my way around the foreign territory of Spanish and Mexican history; of Spanish, Mayan, and Aztec culture and society; and of the national psyche of contemporary Mexico?

About twenty years ago my wife and I were on a short vacation in Quintana Roo and stopped for a brief visit to the seaside village of Akumal. There we saw the striking Ayala sculpture of Gonzalo Guerrero and his family, at that time situated on the beach and facing east into the Caribbean and beyond. A short while later, in the little civic museum in the Cozumel town of San Miguel, we found a brief summary of Guerrero's shipwreck, his absorption into Mayan life and culture, and his fathering of the first *mestizos* in Mexican history. This story was entirely unfamiliar to us—indeed it was unknown to almost any English-speaking visitor. It had been treated in a few scholarly studies outside Mexico, but there were no substantial accounts of it generally available in Canada or the United States. We were struck by the drama of the story—the first encounter in history between the Spanish and the Maya, the remarkable tale of a sixteenth-century European man finding a new life among an indigenous people of America.

As I began to learn more about Guerrero, I became aware of the complexities of his story, particularly his reinvention as a Mayan leader and father. Fascinating questions emerged: why did he not follow Aguilar in joining Cortés, how deeply did he immerse himself in Mayan culture and thought, how much of his Spanish upbringing did he retain, and what did their *mestizo* heritage mean for his children? Most interesting of all was the idea of a merging of European and indigenous cultures, the fundamental underpinning of all of the nations of the Americas, in which there was mutual respect rather than brutal domination of the original inhabitants by the invaders.

All of this was interesting on an intellectual level. But I was also driven by a deeper urge. Is it too fanciful to claim that I was viscerally drawn to a story that had implications for my own life, not that of a Mexican but nonetheless that of a citizen of the Americas? John Ralston Saul would not think so. In 2008, he wrote in *A Fair Country: Telling Truths about Canada* that "we are a métis [mixed race] civilization."[1] He does not mean that all Canadians are Métis, a particular ethnic group that comprises 1.4 per cent of the population, or that all Canadians have some indigenous blood in them. No one knows how many people have aboriginal ancestry, but they are likely to be numerous: my wife's extended family, for example, celebrates its Norwegian roots, but there are at least fifteen members who have aboriginal forebears.

I do not have such forebears. Despite the vigorous searching of several of my close relatives, no evidence of aboriginal blood has ever been found in either my mother's or my father's family tree. Despite living in North America for more than 300 years, my ancestors appear to have remained stoutly northern European. Saul argues, however, that this does not matter because, like all but the newest Canadians, I am métis in my behaviour and thought:

> What we are today has been inspired as much by four centuries of life with the indigenous civilizations as by four centuries of immigration. Perhaps more. Today we are the outcome of that experience.... We increasingly are. This influencing, this shaping, is deep within us.... Whatever our family tree may look like, our intuitions and common sense as a civilization are more Aboriginal than European or African or Asian, even though we have created elaborate theatrical screens of language, reference and mythology to misrepresent ourselves to ourselves.[2]

Author and university administrator Wab Kinew, one of Canada's impressive young aboriginal leaders, makes the same argument, emphasizing what he calls "a simple truth: whether or not you have indigenous blood, if you live in this country, at least part of your identity is indigenous."[3]

Perhaps Saul and Kinew are right: it might be that my self has been misrepresented to me by my education and sociocultural environment, that part of my identity is indeed indigenous. My mother's family members were skilful and knowledgeable woodsmen in the forest and lake country of Muskoka, in Ontario, in the nineteenth century, and my childhood home was full of relics and reminders of that past. My great-grandfather made his own birchbark canoes, and he and all of his children became adept at manoeuvring them over rough lake water, through whitewater rapids, and over long portages. He tramped through Ontario blizzards on snowshoes that he had fashioned from deerhide strips stretched over frames carved from oak or maple, and he was protected from the cold by deerhide moccasins and mitts. To the best of my knowledge, he did not wear a bison-skin coat or survive lean winters on pemmican, as early explorers and western Canadian homesteaders did, but he and his family thrived in a difficult environment by adopting aboriginal ways. I grew up wanting to emulate this familiarity and comfort with the wilderness without ever realizing that my forebears had survived because they had embraced so many indigenous customs and strategies. I wore moccasins—albeit store-bought, commercially made ones—as a child, and I have owned canoes for sixty years without ever thinking about the ancient North American origins of these objects.

Kinew suggests that Canadians who do not recognize that their identity is at least partially aboriginal should "consider the fact that our country has an indigenous name: Kanata."[4] Indeed, when as a child I situated myself in the universe by writing "Saskatoon, Saskatchewan, Canada," I was locating myself—unwittingly I'm afraid—entirely in indigenous terms. This is something that I share with many Mexicans, the name of whose nation comes from "Mēxihco," the Nahuatl term for Tenochtlitán, and it is a reminder that our two countries have much in common in our narratives about our indigenous peoples. Much more in common, in fact, than with the republic that lies between us, known by what Fuentes calls "the name without a name, the ghostlike 'United States of America,' a mere descriptor, like 'Third Floor on the Right.'"[5] For Paz, "in the United States the Indian element does not appear.... The United States was founded in a land without a past. The historical memory of Americans is European, not American, exactly the opposite is true of Mexico, land of superimposed pasts."[6]

In *A Fair Country*, Saul contends that, though Canadian society is very different from Mexican society, the two nations resemble each other in the complexity of their superimposed pasts. In the past few decades, Mexican writers such as Carlos Fuentes, Eugenio Aguirre, Carlos Villa Roiz, Otilia Meza, and others have been part of the larger movement to free their country from the narrative superimposed onto it by four centuries of Spanish military and cultural domination. In the twenty-first century, Canada is profoundly—and often painfully—engaged in a momentous effort to recognize its indigenous identity and redefine a national history "written in English from an anglophone point of view, with its colonial origins, in French from a francophone point of view."[7] In both countries, much of this revision has been undertaken to redress wrongs committed against indigenous peoples and, particularly in Canada, to recognize the rights given to aboriginals several centuries ago. But there is so much more to be gained by everyone, aboriginal and non-aboriginal, in this process: the acceptance of otherness, cultural enrichment, sincere and meaningful dialogue between people who have been kept apart, and perhaps most important of all, a plurality of perspectives. There can be great strength in what aboriginal academic and leader Leroy Little Bear calls "ambidextrous consciousness," a view of the world that is a blend of indigenous and Eurocentric perspectives.[8] Such a fusion of attitudes and cultures could be the foundation of an American reality, a way of seeing and being stretching from Chile to Alaska.

In this context, the story of Gonzalo Guerrero's experience among the Maya, no matter whether one sees it as history or myth, has relevance beyond the Yucatán Peninsula. As a tale of the creation of *mestizos* or métis, or the indigenous identity of all of us in the Americas, it suggests that the values of the New and Old Worlds can be united and accommodated without exploitation and domination. If the legendary Roman Spartacus has come to represent rebellion against slavery, the early Briton King Arthur a chivalric code of service, and the medieval Robin Hood a struggle against the rich and privileged, perhaps the Spanish/Maya

Gonzalo Guerrero can be a hero for the Americas. Someone who embraced the other and embodied a peaceful and equitable fusion of Old and New World values.

ACKNOWLEDGEMENTS

A number of people generously facilitated my travels over the Yucatán Peninsula in search of Gonzalo Guerrero. They include Bill and Diane Mollison, Peter Stoicheff and Katherine Warden, and Gary Goldbaum and Judy Unger. Back home the Interlibrary Loans Department of the University of Saskatchewan Library brought many of the bibliographical traces of Guerrero to my desk.

Mark Abley read an earlier draft of the book with a sensitive critical eye, and his shrewd advice pushed me in interesting directions that I had not considered. Allison Muri's technical expertise rescued a Luddite author at a critical stage, and Rodolfo Pino ensured the accuracy of some critical translations. Most of all, I am grateful to Bruce Walsh and David McLennan, at the University of Regina Press, for recognizing that the story of Guerrero should be read throughout the Americas. David's and Dallas Harrison's careful editing improved the text in many ways.

In the end, my greatest debt is to my wife, Holly. She was with me when, on a sandy beach in Akumal, I first encountered the tale of the shipwrecked Spaniard, and she has been with me all the way as I have tried to fill in the story and understand its meaning. She has, in this and so many other ways, offered unqualified, though never blind, support.

⦿⦿⦿⦿⦿⦿⦿⦿⦿⦿⦿⦿⦿

NOTES

⦿⦿⦿⦿⦿⦿⦿⦿⦿⦿⦿⦿⦿

INTRODUCTION

1   Rolena Adorno, *The Polemics of Possession in Spanish American Narrative* (New Haven, CT: Yale University Press, 2007), 242.

2   Octavio Paz, *The Labyrinth of Solitude and Other Writings*, trans. Lysander Kemp, Yara Milos, and Rachel Phillips Bilash (New York: Grove Press, 1985), 87.

3   Camilla Townsend, *Malintzin's Choices: An Indian Woman in the Conquest of Mexico* (Albuquerque: University of New Mexico Press, 2006), 6.

4   Ibid., 5.

5   Ibid., 2.

6   Ibid., 5, 8.

7   Adorno, *Polemics of Possession*, 242.

CHAPTER ONE

1   Juan Díaz, "Chronicle," in *The Conquistadors: First-Person Accounts of the Conquest of Mexico*, ed. Patricia de Fuentes (New York: Orion Press, 1963), 7.

2   Ronald Wright, *Stolen Continents: Conquest and Resistance in the Americas* (Toronto: Penguin, 2003), 45.

3   Quoted in ibid., 44.

4   John L. Stephens, *Incidents of Travel in Yucatan*, 2 vols. (New York: Dover, 1963), 2: 280.

5   Michel Peissel, *The Lost World of Quintana Roo* (New York: E. P. Dutton, 1963), 53.

6   *Chicleros* were rugged men who tapped the sap of the sapodilla tree, the raw material for chewing gum, deep in the Yucatán jungle.

7   Ibid., 151.

8   Ronald Wright, *Time Among the Maya* (New York: Viking, 1989), 333.

9   The inscription on this statue reflects the commonly held belief, arising from sixteenth-century chronicles, written many years after the event,

that the shipwreck occurred in 1511. However, Kathleen Romoli's authoritative history *Balboa of Darién: Discoverer of the Pacific* (Garden City, NY: Dolphin Books, 1953), 146, states that Guerrero's ship came to grief after setting sail from the Spanish colony of Darién on January 13, 1512.

CHAPTER TWO

1   Romoli, *Balboa of Darién*, 32.

2   Irving A. Leonard, "Introduction," in *The Discovery and Conquest of Mexico: 1517–1521*, by Bernal Díaz del Castillo, trans. A. P. Maudslay, ed. Genero Garcia (New York: Farrar, Straus and Cudahy, 1956), xiii.

3   Quoted in Carlos Fuentes, *The Buried Mirror: Reflections on Spain and the New World* (New York: Houghton Mifflin, 1992), 88.

4   Felipe Fernández-Armesto, *1492: The Year the World Began* (New York: Harper One, 2009), 38.

5   Ibid., 87.

6   Ibid.

7   Christopher Columbus, *The Log of Christopher Columbus*, trans. Robert H. Fuson (Camden, ME: International Marine Publishing Company, 1987), 52.

8   Kirkpatrick Sale, *The Conquest of Paradise: Christopher Columbus and the Columbian Legacy* (New York: Knopf, 1991), 13.

9   Nancy Rubin, *Isabella of Castile: The First Renaissance Queen* (New York: St. Martin's Press, 1991), 329.

10 Francisco López de Gómara, quoted in Hugh Thomas, *Rivers of Gold: The Rise of the Spanish Empire, from Columbus to Magellan* (New York: Random House, 2005), 105.

11 Lewis Hanke, *Bartolomé de las Casas: An Interpretation of His Life and Writings* (The Hague: Martinus Nijhoff, 1951), 9.

12 Sale, *The Conquest of Paradise*, 35.

13 Hugh Thomas, *The Conquest of Mexico* (London: Pimlico, 1994), 58.

14 Díaz del Castillo, *The Discovery and Conquest of Mexico*, 190.

15 Fernández-Armesto, *1492*, 203.

CHAPTER THREE

1   Thomas, *Rivers of Gold*, 212.

2   Eugenio de Salazar, *Seafaring in the Sixteenth Century: The Letter of Eugenio Salazar*, trans. John Frye (San Francisco: Mellen Research University Press, 1991), 29, 31.

3   Ibid., 37.

4   Samuel Eliot Morison, *Admiral of the Ocean Sea: A Life of Christopher Columbus* (New York: MJF Books, 1970), 173.

5   Pablo E. Pérez-Mallaína, *Spain's Men of the Sea: Daily Life in the Indies Fleets in the Sixteenth Century*, trans. Carla Rahn Phillips (Baltimore: Johns Hopkins University Press, 1998), 27.

6   Columbus, quoted in Sale, *The Conquest of Paradise*, 100.

7   Thomas, *Rivers of Gold*, 111.

8   Bartolomé de Las Casas, *The Devastation of the Indies: A Brief Account*, trans. Herma Briffault (Baltimore: Johns Hopkins University Press, 1992), 35.

9   Tzvetan Todorov, *The Conquest of America: The Question of the Other* (New York: Harper Perennial, 1984), 49.

10   Henry Kamen, *Empire: How Spain Became a World Power, 1492–1763* (New York: HarperCollins, 2003), 42.

11   Ibid., 83.

12   Quoted in Thomas, *Rivers of Gold*, 219.

13   Romoli, *Balboa of Darién*, 63.

14   Ibid., 64.

15   Manuel Josef Quintana, *Lives of Vasco Nunez de Balboa and Francisco Pizarro* (London: Blackwood, 1832), 17–18.

16   Thomas, *The Conquest of Mexico*, 57.

17   Romoli, *Balboa of Darién*, 18–19.

18   Alonso Zuazo, quoted in Peter O. Koch, *The Spanish Conquest of the Inca Empire* (London: McFarland and Company, 2008), 16.

19   John Keats, "On First Looking into Chapman's Homer," in *The Poems of John Keats*, ed. Miriam Allott (London: Longman, 1970), 60–61.

CHAPTER FOUR

1   Quoted in Diego de Landa, *Landa's Relación de las cosas de Yucatán*, ed. Alfred M. Tozzer (Cambridge, MA: Peabody Museum, 1941), 29.

2   Díaz del Castillo, *The Discovery and Conquest of Mexico*, 11–12.

3   Ibid., 22–23.

4   Hernán Cortés, *Letters from Mexico*, trans. and ed. Anthony Pagden (New Haven, CT: Yale University Press, 1986), 17.

5   Francisco López de Gómara, *Cortés: The Life of the Conqueror by His Secretary*, trans. and ed. Lesley Byrd Simpson (Berkeley: University of California Press, 1964), 31.

6   Díaz del Castillo, *The Discovery and Conquest of Mexico*, 45.

7   Francisco Cervantes de Salazar, *Crónica de la Nueva España*, in Diego
     de Landa, *Landa's Relación de las cosas de Yucatán*, ed. Alfred M.
     Tozzer (Cambridge, MA: Peabody Museum, 1941), 237.

8   Ibid.

9   Díaz del Castillo, *The Discovery and Conquest of Mexico*, 43.

10   Joseph Conrad, *Heart of Darkness* (London: Penguin Classics, 2000), 112.

11   Bernal Díaz del Castillo, *The History of the Conquest of New Spain*,
     ed. Davíd Carrasco (Albuquerque: University of New Mexico Press,
     2008), 32.

12   Ibid.

13   Inga Clendinnen, *Ambivalent Conquests: Maya and Spaniard in
     Yucatan, 1517–1570* (Cambridge, UK: Cambridge University Press,
     1987), 18.

14   López de Gómara, *Cortés*, 32.

15   Cervantes de Salazar, *Crónica de la Nueva España*, 236.

16   Gonzalo Fernández de Oviedo, *Historia general y natural de las Indias*,
     vol. 3 (Madrid: Ediciones Atlas, 1959), 404, 405.

17   Clendinnen, *Ambivalent Conquests*, 18.

18   Washington Irving, *Companions of Columbus* (Boston: Twayne, 1986),
     165, 169–70.

19   Clendinnen, *Ambivalent Conquests*, 18.

20   Quoted in López de Gómara, *Cortés*, 32.

21   Díaz del Castillo, *The Discovery and Conquest of Mexico*, 46.

22   Clendinnen, *Ambivalent Conquests*, 18.

CHAPTER FIVE

1   J. Eric S. Thompson, *Maya History and Religion* (Norman: University of
     Oklahoma Press, 1990), 127.

2   Susan Kepecs and Rani T. Alexander, eds., *The Post-Classic to Spanish
     Era Transition in Mesoamerica* (Albuquerque: University of New
     Mexico Press, 2005), 124.

3   Landa, *Landa's Relación de las cosas de Yucatán*, 89–90.

4   Ibid., 90–91.

5   Ibid.

6   Fray Diego Durán, *Book of the Gods and Rites and the Ancient
     Calendar*, trans. and ed. Fernando Horcasitas and Doris Heyden
     (Norman: University of Oklahoma Press, 1971), 270.

7   Victor von Hagen, *World of the Maya* (New York: New American
     Library, 1960), 131.

8   Landa, *Landa's Relación de las cosas de Yucatán*, 110–11.

CHAPTER SIX

1   Cited in J. H. Elliott, *Imperial Spain: 1469–1716* (London: Penguin, 1990), 128.
2   Las Casas, *History of the Indies*, 192–93.
3   Ibid., 193.
4   Stephen Greenblatt, *Marvelous Possessions: The Wonder of the New World* (Chicago: University of Chicago Press, 1991), 98.
5   Las Casas, *History of the Indies*, 196.
6   Townsend, *Malintzin's Choices*, 58.
7   Díaz del Castillo, *The Discovery and Conquest of Mexico*, 46.
8   Ibid., 60.
9   Ibid.
10   Ibid., 61.
11   Ibid., 229.
12   López de Gómara, *Cortés*, 33.
13   Díaz del Castillo, *The Discovery and Conquest of Mexico*, 103.
14   Ibid., 104.
15   Ibid., 153.
16   Ibid., 106.
17   Ibid., 333–34.
18   Ibid., 365.
19   Ibid., 376.
20   Ibid., 377.
21   R. C. Padden, *The Hummingbird and the Hawk* (New York: Harper Colophon, 1967), 230.
22   Karen Vieira Powers, *Women in the Crucible of Conquest* (Albuquerque: University of New Mexico Press, 2005), 69.
23   Díaz del Castillo, *The Discovery and Conquest of Mexico*, 63, 64.
24   Townsend, *Malintzin's Choices*, 6.
25   Díaz del Castillo, *The Discovery and Conquest of Mexico*, 64.
26   López de Gómara, *Cortés*, 56.
27   Cortés, *Letters from Mexico*, 73.
28   López de Gómara, *Cortés*, 408.
29   Townsend, *Malintizin's Choices*, 180, 181.
30   Landa, *Landa's Relación de las cosas de Yucatán*, 29, note.

CHAPTER SEVEN

1   Clendinnen, *Ambivalent Conquests*, 8.
2   López de Gómara, *Cortés*, 58.
3   Díaz del Castillo, *The Discovery and Conquest of Mexico*, 130.

4   Ibid., 54.

5   Clendinnen, *Ambivalent Conquests*, 27.

6   Díaz del Castillo, *The Discovery and Conquest of Mexico*, 58.

7   Ibid., 46.

8   Quoted in Robert S. Chamberlain, *The Conquest and Colonization of Yucatan* (Washington, DC: Carnegie Institution, 1948), 34.

9   Gonzalo Fernández de Oviedo, *Historia general y natural de las Indias*, vol. 3 (Madrid: Ediciones Atlas, 1959), 404–05.

10 Ibid., 405.

11 Ibid., 404, 405.

12 Chamberlain, *The Conquest and Colonization of Yucatan*, 171.

13 Ibid., 63–64.

14 Quoted in ibid., 102.

15 Quoted in ibid., 235.

16 Quoted in Landa, *Landa's Relación de las cosas de Yucatán*, 8.

17 Chamberlain, *The Conquest and Colonization of Yucatan*, 338–39.

CHAPTER EIGHT

1   Manuel Aguilar-Morena and Erika Cabrera, *Diego Rivera: A Biography* (Santa Barbara: Greenwood, 2011), 86.

2   Sandra Messinger Cypess, "'Mother' Malinche and Allegories of Gender, Ethnicity, and National Identity in Mexico," in *Feminism, Nation, and Myth: La Malinche*, ed. Rolando Romero and Amanda Nolacea Harris (Houston: Arte Público Press, 2005), 21–22.

3   Fernández de Oviedo, *Historia general y natural de las Indias* 3: 404–05.

4   López de Gómara, *Cortés*, 32.

5   Cervantes de Salazar, *Crónica de la Nueva España*, 236.

6   Moisés González Navarro, "*Mestizaje* in Mexico during the National Period," in *Race and Class in Latin America*, ed. Magnus Mörner (New York: Columbia University Press, 1970), 145.

7   Carlos Fuentes, *The Buried Mirror: Reflections on Spain and the New World* (Boston: Houghton Mifflin, 1992), 117.

8   Carlos Fuentes, *The Orange Tree*, trans. Alfred MacAdam (New York: Harper Perennial, 1994), 47.

9   Mario Aguirre Rosas, *Gonzalo de Guerrero: Padre del mestizaje iberoamericano* (Mexico City: Editorial Jus, 1975).

10 Roseanna Mueller, "From Cult to Comics: The Representation of Gonzalo Guerrero as Cultural Hero in Mexican Popular Culture," in *A Twice-Told Tale: Reinventing the Encounter in Iberian/Iberian American*

Literature and Film, ed. Santiago Juan-Navarro and Theodore Robert Young (Newark: University of Delaware Press, 2001), 146.

11 Quoted in ibid.

12 Quoted in Adorno, *Polemics of Possession*, 243.

13 Ibid., 244.

14 Quoted in Mueller, "From Cult to Comics," 141.

15 Eugenio Aguirre, *Gonzalo Guerrero: Novela histórica* (México: Universidad Nacional Autónoma de México, 1980), 223–24.

16 Mark A. Hernández, *Figural Conquistadors: Rewriting the New World's Discovery and Conquest in Mexican and River Plate Novels of the 1980s and 1990s* (Lewisburg, PA: Bucknell University Press, 2006), 91.

17 Otilia Meza, *Immortal Love: Gonzalo Guerrero, Symbol of the Origin of Mexican Miscegenation (Historical Novel)* (Mexico City: Alpe, 1994), 140.

18 Carlos Villa Roiz, *Gonzalo Guerrero: Memoria olvidada, trauma de México* (México: Plaza y Valdés, 1995), 22.

19 Ibid., 499.

20 Ibid., 568.

21 Alan Clark, *Guerrero and Heart's Blood* (Mexico City: Serpiente, 1999).

22 John Curl, "Homage to Gonzalo Guerrero," in *Scorched Birth: Poetry*, by John Curl (Berkeley: Beatitude Press, 2006), 55.

23 Anita Mason, *The Right Hand of the Sun* (London: John Murray, 2008), 329.

24 Ibid., 358.

25 John Coe Robbins, *Maya Lord* (Jersey City, NJ: Whiskey Creek Press, 2011).

26 Alfonso Mateo-Sagasta, *Caminarás con el sol* (Barcelona: Grijalbo/Random House/Mondadori, 2011), 21.

27 Ibid., 13.

28 Ibid., 39.

29 Alfonso Mateo-Sagasta, "Guerrero fue un traidor en su época, pero hoy lo entendemos," http://www. elperiodicodearagon.com/noticias/alfonso-mateo-sagasta-guerrero.

30 Victoria E. Campos, "Toward a New History: Twentieth-Century Debates in Mexico on Narrating the National Past," in *A Twice-Told Tale: Reinventing the Encounter in Iberian/Iberian American Literature and Film*, ed. Santiago Juan-Navarro and Theodore Robert Young (Newark: University of Delaware Press, 2001), 50.

31 John Ralston Saul, *The Comeback: How Aboriginals Are Reclaiming Power and Influence* (Toronto: Viking, 2014), 11.

32 "Spaniard Gonzalo Guerrero Shapes Maya Future in 16th Century," *USA Today Mexican Caribbean Edition*, February 19, 2010, MC1.

33 Ramón Iván Suárez Caamal, "Hymn to Quintana Roo," 1985.

34 Paz, *The Labyrinth of Solitude and Other Writings*, 20.

35 Rolando Romero, "Texts, Pre-Texts, Con-Texts: Gonzalo Guerrero in the Chronicles of the Indies," *Revista de estudios hispánicos* 29, 3 (1992): 363.

36 Cypess, "'Mother' Malinche," 20–21, 22, 25.

37 Townsend, *Malintzin's Choices*, 2.

AFTERWORD

1 John Ralston Saul, *A Fair Country: Telling Truths about Canada* (Toronto: Viking, 2008), 3.

2 Ibid.

3 Annette Trimbee and Wab Kinew, "Canada's Universities Should Mandate Indigenous Courses," *Globe and Mail*, December 10, 2015, A16.

4 Ibid.

5 Carlos Fuentes, *The Crystal Frontier*, trans. Alfred MacAdam (New York: Farrar, Straus and Giroux, 1997), 65.

6 Paz, *The Labyrinth of Solitude and Other Writings*, 362.

7 Quoted in Saul, *A Fair Country*, 21.

8 Leroy Little Bear, "Jagged Worldviews Colliding," in *Reclaiming Indigenous Voice and Vision*, ed. Marie Battiste (Vancouver: UBC Press, 2000), 85.

BIBLIOGRAPHY

Abulafia, David. *The Discovery of Mankind: Atlantic Encounters in the Age of Columbus*. New Haven, CT: Yale University Press, 2008.

Adorno, Rolena. *The Polemics of Possession in Spanish American Narrative*. New Haven, CT: Yale University Press, 2007.

Aguilar-Morena, Manuel, and Erika Cabrera. *Diego Rivera: A Biography*. Santa Barbara: Greenwood, 2011.

Aguirre, Eugenio. *Gonzalo Guerrero: Novela histórica*. México: Universidad Nacional Autónoma de México, 1980.

Bown, Stephen R. *1494: How a Family Feud in Medieval Spain Divided the World in Half*. New York: St. Martin's Press, 2011.

Bradford, Ernle. *Christopher Columbus*. New York: Viking Press, 1973.

Campos, Victoria E. "Toward a New History: Twentieth-Century Debates in Mexico on Narrating the National Past." In *A Twice-Told Tale: Reinventing the Encounter in Iberian/Iberian American Literature and Film*, edited by Santiago Juan-Navarro and Theodore Robert Young, 47–64. Newark: University of Delaware Press, 2001.

Castro Pacheco, Fernando. *Murales del Palacio de Gobierno*. Mérida: Offset Rebosan, 2005.

Ceballos y Borjas, Jose Armando. *Gonzalo Guerrero: Apuntes para su biografía*. Chetumal: Fondo de Fomento Editorial del Gobierno del Estado de Quintana Roo, n.d.

Cerwin, Herbert. *Bernal Diaz: Historian of the Conquest*. Norman: University of Oklahoma Press, 1963.

Chamberlain, Robert S. *The Conquest and Colonization of Honduras: 1502–1550*. Washington, DC: Carnegie Institution, 1953.

———. *The Conquest and Colonization of Yucatan*. Washington, DC: Carnegie Institution, 1948.

Clark, Alan. *Guerrero and Heart's Blood*. Mexico City: Serpiente, 1999.

Clendinnen, Inga. *Ambivalent Conquests: Maya and Spaniard in Yucatan, 1517–1570*. Cambridge, UK: Cambridge University Press, 1987.

Coe, Michael D. *The Maya*. London: Thames and Hudson, 2005.

Columbus, Christopher. *The Log of Christopher Columbus*. Translated by Robert H. Fuson. Camden, ME: International Marine Publishing Company, 1987.

Conrad, Joseph. *Heart of Darkness*. London: Penguin Classics, 2000.

Cortés, Hernán. *Letters from Mexico*. Translated and edited by Anthony Pagden. New Haven, CT: Yale University Press, 1986.

Cowie, Lancelot. "Gonzalo Guerrero: Historical and Literary Figure of the Conquest of Mexico." *American Notebooks: New Age* 2, 144 (2013): 185–204.

Curl, John. "Homage to Gonzalo Guerrero." In *Scorched Birth: Poetry, by John Curl*, 55. Berkeley: Beatitude Press, 2006.

Cypess, Sandra Messinger. "'Mother' Malinche and Allegories of Gender, Ethnicity, and National Identity in Mexico." In *Feminism, Nation, and Myth: La Malinche*, edited by Rolando Romero and Amanda Nolacea Harris, 14–27. Houston: Arte Público Press, 2005.

Díaz, Juan. "Chronicle." In *The Conquistadors: First-Person Accounts of the Conquest of Mexico*, edited by Patricia de Fuentes, 3–16. New York: Orion Press, 1963.

Díaz del Castillo, Bernal. *The Discovery and Conquest of Mexico: 1517-1521*. Translated by A. P. Maudslay. Edited by Genero Garcia. New York: Farrar, Straus and Cudahy, 1956.

———. *The History of the Conquest of New Spain*. Edited by Davíd Carrasco. Albuquerque: University of New Mexico Press, 2008.

Diccionario Porrúa de historia, biografía, y geografía de Mexico. México: Editorial Porrúa, 1964.

Domingo, Rosa Pellicer. "El cautivo cautivado: Gonzalo Guerrero en la novela mexicana del siglo XX." *América sin nombre* 9–10 (2007): 157–66.

Dorantes de Carranza, Baltasar. *Sumeria relación de las cosas de la Nueva España*. México: Editorial Porrúa, 1987.

Durán, Fray Diego. *Book of the Gods and Rites and the Ancient Calendar*. Translated and edited by Fernando Horcasitas and Doris Heyden. Norman: University of Oklahoma Press, 1971.

———. *The History of the Indies of New Spain*. Translated by Doris Heyden. Norman: University of Oklahoma Press, 1994.

Earle, Rebecca. *The Body of the Conquistador: Food, Race, and the Colonial Experience in Spanish America, 1492-1700*. Cambridge, UK: Cambridge University Press, 2012.

Edwards, John. *The Spain of the Catholic Monarchs, 1474-1520*. Oxford: Blackwell Publishers, 2000.

Elliott, J. H. *Imperial Spain: 1469–1716*. London: Penguin, 1990.

Fernández de Oviedo, Gonzalo. *Historia general y natural de las Indias*. Vol. 3. Madrid: Ediciones Atlas, 1959.

———. *Writing from the Edge of the World: The Memoirs of Darién, 1514–1527*. Tuscaloosa: University of Alabama Press, 2006.

Fernández-Armesto, Felipe. *1492: The Year the World Began*. New York: Harper One, 2009.

Fuentes, Carlos. *The Buried Mirror: Reflections on Spain and the New World*. Boston: Houghton Mifflin, 1992.

———. *The Crystal Frontier*. Translated by Alfred MacAdam. New York: Farrar, Straus and Giroux, 1997.

———. *The Orange Tree*. Translated by Alfred MacAdam. New York: Harper Perennial, 1994.

Garrison, Omar V. *Balboa: Conquistador: The Soul-Odyssey of Vasco Núñez, Discoverer of the Pacific*. New York: Lyle Stuart, 1971.

Gonzalo Guerrero. Akumal: Club de Yates, n.d.

Greenblatt, Stephen. *Marvelous Possessions: The Wonder of the New World*. Chicago: University of Chicago Press, 1991.

Hanke, Lewis. *Bartolomé de las Casas: An Interpretation of His Life and Writings*. The Hague: Martinus Nijhoff, 1951.

Henderson, John S. *The World of the Ancient Maya*. Ithaca, NY: Cornell University Press, 1981.

Hernández, Mark A. *Figural Conquistadors: Rewriting the New World's Discovery and Conquest in Mexican and River Plate Novels of the 1980s and 1990s*. Lewisburg, PA: Bucknell University Press, 2006.

Himmerich y Valencia, Robert. *The Encomenderos of New Spain: 1521–1555*. Translated by Joseph P. Sánchez. Austin: University of Texas Press, 1991.

Irving, Washington. *Companions of Columbus*. Boston: Twayne, 1986.

———. *Voyages and Discoveries of the Companions of Christopher Columbus*. Edited by James W. Tuttleton. Boston: Twayne, 1986.

Horgan, Paul. *Conquistadors in North American History*. New York: Farrar, Straus and Giroux, 1963.

Howarth, David. *The Golden Isthmus*. London: Collins, 1966.

Innes, Hammond. *The Conquistadors*. New York: Knopf, 1969.

Johnson, William Weber. *Cortés: Conquering the New World*. New York: Paragon House, 1987.

Jones, Grant D. *Maya Resistance to Spanish Rule*. Albuquerque: University of New Mexico Press, 1989.

Kamen, Henry. *Empire: How Spain Became a World Power, 1492–1763*. New York: HarperCollins, 2003.

Karttunen, Frances. *Between Worlds: Interpreters, Guides, and Survivors.* New Brunswick, NJ: Rutgers University Press, 1994.

Keats, John. "On First Looking into Chapman's Homer." In *The Poems of John Keats*, edited by Miriam Allott, 60–61. London: Longman, 1970.

Kepecs, Susan, and Rani T. Alexander, eds. *The Post-Classic to Spanish Era Transition in Mesoamerica.* Albuquerque: University of New Mexico Press, 2005.

Koch, Peter O. *The Spanish Conquest of the Inca Empire.* London: McFarland and Company, 2008.

Landa, Diego de. *Landa's Relación de las cosas de Yucatán.* Translated and edited by Alfred M. Tozzer. Cambridge, MA: Peabody Museum, 1941.

Las Casas, Bartolomé de. *The Devastation of the Indies: A Brief Account.* Translated by Herma Briffault. Baltimore: Johns Hopkins University Press, 1992.

———. *History of the Indies.* Translated and edited by Andrée Collard. New York: Harper Torchbooks, 1971.

Laughton, Timothy. *The Maya: Life, Myth, and Art.* London: Duncan Baird Publishers, 1998.

Lipschutz, Alejandro. *El problema racial en la conquista de America y el mestizaje.* Santiago: Editora Austral, 1963.

Liss, Peggy K. *Mexico under Spain, 1521–1556.* Chicago: University of Chicago Press, 1975.

Little Bear, Leroy. "Jagged Worldviews Colliding." In *Reclaiming Indigenous Voice and Vision*, edited by Marie Battiste, 77–85. Vancouver: UBC Press, 2000.

López de Gómara, Francisco. *Cortés: The Life of the Conqueror by His Secretary.* Translated and edited by Lesley Byrd Simpson. Berkeley: University of California Press, 1964.

MacQuarrie, Kim. *The Last Days of the Inca.* New York: Simon and Schuster, 2007.

Madariaga, Salvador de. *Hernán Cortés: Conqueror of Mexico.* London: Hodder and Stoughton, 1941.

Mann, Charles C. *1491: New Revelations of the Americas before Columbus.* New York: Vintage Books, 2005.

Mason, Anita. *The Right Hand of the Sun.* London: John Murray, 2008.

Mateo-Sagasta, Alfonso. *Caminarás con el sol.* Barcelona: Grijalbo/Random House/Mondadori, 2011.

———. "Guerrero fue un traidor en su época, pero hoy lo entendemos." http://www. elperiodicodearagon.com/noticias/alfonso-mateo-sagasta-guerrero.

May, Antoinette. *The Yucatan: A Guide to the Land of Maya Mysteries*. San Carlos: Wide World Publishing, 1993.

Meza, Otilia. *Un amor inmortal: Gonzalo Guerrero, símbolo del origen del mestizaje mexicano (novella histórica)*. Mexico City: Alpe, 1994.

Morison, Samuel Eliot. *Admiral of the Ocean Sea: A Life of Christopher Columbus*. New York: MJF Books, 1970.

Mueller, RoseAnna. "From Cult to Comics: The Representation of Gonzalo Guerrero as Cultural Hero in Mexican Popular Culture." In *A Twice-Told Tale: Reinventing the Encounter in Iberian/Iberian American Literature and Film*, edited by Santiago Juan-Navarro and Theodore Robert Young, 137–48. Newark: University of Delaware Press, 2001.

Navarro, Moisés González. "*Mestizaje* in Mexico during the National Period." In *Race and Class in Latin America*, edited by Magnus Mörner, 145–69. New York: Columbia University Press, 1970.

Operé, Fernando. *Indian Captivity in Spanish America: Frontier Narratives*. Translated by Gustavo Pellón. Charlottesville: University of Virginia Press, 2008.

Oxford Encyclopedia of Mesoamerican Cultures. Vol. 1. Oxford: Oxford University Press, 2001.

Padden, R. C. *The Hummingbird and the Hawk*. New York: Harper Colophon, 1967.

Parry, J. H. *The Discovery of South America*. New York: Taplinger, 1979.

Paz, Octavio. *The Labyrinth of Solitude and Other Writings*. Translated by Lysander Kemp, Yara Milos, and Rachel Phillips Bilash. New York: Grove Press, 1985.

Peissel, Michel. *The Lost World of Quintana Roo*. New York: E. P. Dutton, 1963.

Pérez-Mallaina, Pablo E. *Spain's Men of the Sea: Daily Life in the Indies Fleets in the Sixteenth Century*. Translated by Carla Rahn Phillips. Baltimore: Johns Hopkins University Press, 1998.

Powers, Karen Vieira. *Women in the Crucible of Conquest*. Albuquerque: University of New Mexico Press, 2005.

Prescott, William H. *Conquest of Mexico*. Reprinted, New York: Book League of America, 1934.

———. *History of the Reign of Ferdinand and Isabella the Catholic*. New York: Harper and Brothers, 1845.

Quintana, Manuel Josef. *Lives of Vasco Nunez de Balboa and Francisco Pizarro*. London: Blackwood, 1832.

Restall, Matthew. *Maya Conquistador*. Boston: Beacon Press, 1998.

——. *Seven Myths of the Spanish Conquest*. Oxford: Oxford University Press, 2003.

Reston, James Jr. *Dogs of God: Columbus, the Inquisition, and the Defeat of the Moors*. New York: Anchor, 2005.

Ricard, Robert. *The Spiritual Conquest of Mexico*. Translated by Lesley Byrd Simpson. Berkeley: University of California Press, 1982.

Rico, José. "Gonzalo Guerrero in the Border of the Spanish Imagination." http://biblioteca.clacso.edu.ar/libros/lasa97/.

Robbins, John Coe. *Maya Lord*. Jersey City: Whiskey Creek Press, 2011.

Romero, Rolando. "Texts, Pre-Texts, Con-Texts: Gonzalo Guerrero in the Chronicles of the Indies." *Revista de estudios hispánicos* 29 3 (1992): 345–67.

Romero, Rolando, and Amanda Nolacea Harris, eds. *Feminism, Nation, and Myth: La Malinche*. Houston: Arte Público Press, 2005.

Romoli, Kathleen. *Balboa of Darién: Discoverer of the Pacific*. Garden City, NY: Dolphin Books, 1953.

Rosas, Mario Aguirre. *Gonzalo de Guerrero: Padre del mestizaje iberoamericano*. Mexico City: Editorial Jus, 1975.

Roys, Ralph L. *The Political Geography of the Yucatan Maya*. Washington, DC: Carnegie Institution, 1957.

Rubin, Nancy. *Isabella of Castile: The First Renaissance Queen*. New York: St. Martin's Press, 1991.

Sahagún, Bernadino de. *The Conquest of New Spain*. Salt Lake City: University of Utah Press, 1989.

Salazar, Cervantes de. *Crónica de la Nueva España*. In *Landa's Relación de las cosas de Yucatán*, by Diego de Landa, edited by Alfred M. Tozzer, 233–39. Cambridge, MA: Peabody Museum, 1941.

Salazar, Eugenio de. *Seafaring in the Sixteenth Century: The Letter of Eugenio Salazar*. Translated by John Frye. San Francisco: Mellen Research University Press, 1991.

Sale, Kirkpatrick. *The Conquest of Paradise: Christopher Columbus and the Columbian Legacy*. New York: Knopf, 1990.

Sauer, Carl Ortwin. *The Early Spanish Main*. Berkeley: University of California Press, 1966.

Saul, John Ralston. *The Comeback: How Aboriginals Are Reclaiming Power and Influence*. Toronto: Viking, 2014.

——. *A Fair Country: Telling Truths about Canada*. Toronto: Viking, 2008.

Schele, Linda, and Peter Mathews. *The Code of Kings: The Language of Seven Sacred Maya Temples and Tombs*. New York: Scribner, 1998.

Schlesinger, Victoria. *Animals and Plants of the Ancient Maya: A Guide.* Austin: University of Texas Press, 2001.

Schroeder, Susan, Anne J. Cruz, Cristián Roa-de-la-Carrera, and David E. Tavárez, trans. and eds. *Chimalpahin's Conquest: A Nahua Historian's Rewriting of Francisco López de Gómara's* La conquista de México. Stanford: Stanford University Press, 2010.

"Spaniard Gonzalo Guerrero Shapes Maya Future in 16th Century." USA *Today Mexican Caribbean Edition*, February 19, 2010, MC1.

Stephens, John L. *Incidents of Travel in Yucatan.* 2 vols. New York: Dover, 1963.

Stuart, Gene S., and George E. Stuart. *Lost Kingdoms of the Maya.* Washington, DC: National Geographic Society, 1993.

Suárez Caamal, Ramón Iván. "Hymn to Quintana Roo." 1985.

Thomas, Hugh. *The Conquest of Mexico.* London: Pimlico, 1994.

———. *Rivers of Gold: The Rise of the Spanish Empire from Columbus to Magellan.* New York: Random House, 2005.

Thompson, J. Eric S. *Maya History and Religion.* Norman: University of Oklahoma Press, 1990.

Todorov, Tzvetan. *The Conquest of America: The Question of the Other.* New York: HarperPerennial, 1984.

Townsend, Camilla. *Malintzin's Choices: An Indian Woman in the Conquest.* Albuquerque: University of New Mexico Press, 2006.

Trimbee, Annette, and Wab Kinew. "Canada's Universities Should Mandate Indigenous Courses." *Globe and Mail*, December 10, 2015, A16.

von Hagen, Victor. *World of the Maya.* New York: New American Library, 1960.

Villa Roiz, Carlos. *Gonzalo Guerrero: Memoria olvidada, trauma de México.* México: Plaza y Valdés, 1995.

Wood, Michael. *Conquistadors.* Berkeley: University of California Press, 2000.

Wright, Ronald. *Stolen Continents: Conquest and Resistance in the Americas.* Toronto: Penguin, 2003.

———. *Time Among the Maya.* New York: Viking, 1989.

INDEX

 Robert Calder is Emeritus Professor of English from the University of Saskatchewan. Considered by many to be the leading authority in the world on the English author William Somerset Maugham, he is the author of *W. Somerset Maugham and the Quest for Freedom* and *Willie: The Life of W. Somerset Maugham*, which won the 1989 Governor General's Literary Award for Non-Fiction. His other books include *Beware the British Serpent: The Role of Writers in British Propaganda in the United States, 1939–1945*, which won two Saskatchewan Book Awards in 2004, and *A Richer Dust: Family, Memory and the Second World War*, winner of the 2003 John V. Hicks Long Manuscript Award.

Throughout his academic career, Calder has travelled regularly to the Yucatan, along the way assembling research on Gonzalo Guerrero on each visit, as his fascination at his discovery grew into an obsession.